THE ROAD TO FORGIVENESS

Letting Go, Letting God, and Learning to Live Again

Innocent B. Maluka

Kingdom Teacher

Printed by Verse Connect

Printed in South Africa

A book template by Used to Tech (https://usedtotech.com)

Available from Amazon.com and other retail outlets

First Printing Edition, 2021

ISBN: 978-0-620-95540-9

EPUB: 978-0-620-95236-1-1

Contents

Dedication and Acknowledgement

This book is dedicated first to our Lord and Savior, Jesus Christ. He is the One who steps into our mess, lifts the weight we cannot carry, and heals what we didn't even know was broken. His blood speaks louder than every hurt and every memory, and His mercy always reaches us before judgment ever could.

Jesus, thank You for forgiving us again and again, for walking with us while we learn, and for giving us the grace to forgive others even when it's hard. Every bit of hope in these pages comes from You, and every bit of glory goes back to You.

I must thank my awesome wife, Mmathapelo Maluka. For all her motivation and support throughout my work. The wisdom she has shared during this writing is gold to me and all the readers of this book. From reading and editing my work to playing with our son so that I may have enough time and space to focus on finishing this book, she is as vital to completing this book as I was. Thank you so much, Shugu.

Preface

O ne of the clearest ways God shows us what He wants us to do is through the things He places heavy on our hearts. The things that bother us. The things we cannot shake no matter how hard we try. We do not always understand why a certain burden shows up, but we recognize when God is pushing us toward something that needs our obedience.

My own moment came quietly. It happened when I started paying attention to how many people walk around carrying pain every single day. Smiling on the outside while their hearts bleed on the inside. People going to work, raising families, serving in church, giving their best, and still carrying wounds that were never treated. Disappointments they never talked about. Betrayals they never healed from. The more I listened in conversations, counseling sessions, and testimonies shared with shaking voices, the more I realized something. Forgiveness is not a small message. It can literally save a life.

As people opened up, I noticed a pattern. Many were not hurting because of something recent. They were hurting because of something old that never healed. Some had been carrying pain for years. Others had built their whole lives around that hurt. They wanted freedom, but they did not know where to start. They loved God, but still felt trapped by emotions they could not explain or control.

That is when God began stirring something in me. It was

simple but strong. His people are wounded, and many do not know how to be healed.

Forgiveness is one of the greatest gifts God has given us, yet it is also one of the hardest things to walk out. It goes against how we feel. It challenges our pride. It touches our deepest pain. It asks us to be honest, humble, and brave. And for many people, forgiveness feels like losing. In truth, it is the doorway to getting your life back.

I wrote this book because I believe there is real beauty on the other side of hurt. Not because pain itself is beautiful, but because God can bring beauty out of anything we give Him. If He can redeem our sins and restore what is broken, He can lead us into forgiveness too.

Just like Finding Beauty in Marriage was written to lift up love, unity, and purpose, this book was written to lift up healing, restoration, and freedom. It does not pretend pain is not real. It looks at pain with truth, compassion, and hope. It is "pro forgiveness," not because it is easy, but because it is necessary if you want to be whole.

My prayer is that by the time you finish this book, you will see forgiveness differently. Not as something forced on you. Not as something you have to do to be a "good Christian." But as something God offers you because He loves you. A gift meant to give you back your joy, renew your strength, and set your heart free.

May this journey open your eyes, lift your spirit, and lead you toward the beauty waiting on the other side of healing. This is the most intentional forgiveness book you will ever read. I pray God uses it to bring light into the places you have kept hidden, and that your heart finally finds the freedom it has been longing for.

INNOCENT B. MALUKA

The Road to Forgiveness

Introduction

Hurt is something every person knows. It does not matter where you come from or how strong you look on the outside. Life has a way of touching the tender parts of your heart. Sometimes the hurt is small. A misunderstanding. A careless comment. A hope that did not turn out the way you thought it would. Other times the hurt is so deep that it shakes who you are and how you see others.

What makes pain feel heavier is that it usually comes from people we trusted. People we opened our lives to. People who knew the parts of us we did not show to anyone else. Whether it is a spouse, a parent, a friend, a sibling, someone at work, or someone we once called family, wounds from close relationships tend to cut the deepest.

Here is the part many of us wrestle with. Life will hurt us, but it is our response that decides whether we heal or keep bleeding on the inside. Some of us build walls. Some pull back from everyone. Some become angry. Some pretend they are fine even when they are not. Some pray but still feel stuck. Some say they forgive, but their hearts stay locked up.

And without noticing it, many people carry old pain into new seasons. They try to love, but fear steps in. They try to trust, but memories rise up. They try to move forward, but something inside keeps pulling them back. Forgiveness is often the missing link. Not because it erases the past. Not because it makes what happened acceptable. Not because it means you lost. Forgiveness matters because it gives you your power back.

God never created forgiveness to weigh us down. He created it to set us free. When Jesus spoke about forgiveness, He was not giving us a rule to follow. He was placing a weapon in our hands, a spiritual weapon strong enough to tear down bitterness, remove shame, and break the emotional prisons we sometimes build around ourselves.

As you go through this book, you will see that we do not rush the process. You will not be told to "just get over it." Your pain will not be brushed aside. Healing takes time. Forgiveness is not a quick moment. It is a journey. A slow, intentional, sometimes uncomfortable journey. But it is also a beautiful one because it leads you back to God's heart.

You will learn that forgiveness brings peace back to your mind. It protects your joy. It cleans your spirit. It releases you from the emotional debt you were never meant to carry. This book is not about pretending everything is fine.

It is about being honest about where it hurts and bringing that hurt into the light of God's Word, allowing His Spirit to walk with you step by step. Just as marriage has a pattern that leads to beauty, forgiveness has a pattern that leads to freedom. The God who heals marriages also heals hearts. The God who restores relationships also restores souls. And the God who teaches us how to love also teaches us how to forgive.

You may be holding this book with a heavy heart. Maybe you are unsure if healing is possible or if you can ever feel whole again. I want you to know something. Your healing is possible. And by simply opening this book and taking this step, it has already begun.

If you have the courage to walk the road of forgiveness, God has the grace to meet you at every step. Welcome to your healing journey. Let us walk this road together.

Chapter 1: When Love Hurts: Naming Your Wound

H urt is one of those uninvited guests that walks into life without knocking, without warning, and without asking permission. It slips into the heart quietly at first, then settles in until the weight becomes too heavy to ignore.

Sometimes the wound arrives loudly, with words spoken in anger or acts of betrayal that cut deep in a moment. Other times it comes slowly, through disappointments that pile up over time, through unmet expectations, broken promises, or moments when the people you trust most fail to be who you thought they were. However it comes, hurt never leaves the heart the same.

When Love Becomes the Source of Pain

There is a unique kind of pain that comes when the person who hurts you is someone you love. It is one thing to be offended by a stranger. It is something completely different when the wound comes from a spouse, a parent, a child, a sibling, a friend, or someone you once treated like family.

Love opens the door to vulnerability. Vulnerability opens the door to risk. When someone has access to your heart, they reach the parts of you that are not guarded by walls, masks, or pretence. It is in these unprotected places that hurt strikes the hardest. When love and trust are involved, the pain feels personal, sharp, and deeply disarming.

Bleeding in Silence

Many people move through life bleeding on the inside while functioning on the outside. They smile, greet, serve, work, and even worship. From a distance they look fine.

Yet somewhere inside, out of sight, something still aches. Something still feels broken. Something still feels stolen. Life carries on, but it feels heavier than it should. Joy feels distant. Peace feels unfamiliar. It is not because they do not love God. It is not because they have no faith. It is because the heart is not healed yet. And an unhealed heart quietly touches everything around it.

The First Step: Naming the Wound

Healing does not begin until the wound has a name. You cannot overcome what you never identify. You cannot surrender what you refuse to acknowledge.

Many people struggle with forgiveness, not because they are stubborn, but because they do not fully understand what they need to forgive. Some have pushed the memory down for so long that they no longer know where to start. Others know exactly what happened, but speaking it feels like touching fire with bare hands. They fear that if they talk about it, they will fall apart.

Naming the wound feels risky, but it is essential. Hidden pain shapes a life more than the pain that is brought into the light.

God With the Brokenhearted

Psalm 34:18 tells me that the Lord is close to the brokenhearted and that He saves those who are crushed in spirit.

This shows me two things. First, God sees the brokenhearted. He does not ignore their pain or brush it aside. Second, brokenness does not push Him away. It draws Him near.

He is closest when you feel most wounded, most overwhelmed, and most defeated. That means naming your wound is not a lonely road. God is already near, ready to walk with you through every emotion, every memory, and every layer of truth that rises to the surface.

Honesty Is Not Weakness

Sometimes the first step toward naming the wound is as simple as admitting that you are hurt. Many believers struggle with this. They worry that speaking about their pain makes them look weak, immature, or lacking faith. But admitting pain is not unbelief. It is honesty.

Even Jesus expresses pain. He weeps at Lazarus' tomb. His soul is troubled in Gethsemane. He cries out from the cross. He does not pretend to be untouched by sorrow. If the Son of God does not hide His hurt, why do we, with all our fragility, try to convince ourselves that nothing affects us?

When Pretending Delays Healing

Pretending you are not hurting does not protect you. It delays your healing. Pushed-down pain does not disappear. It finds new ways to speak. It shows up in overreactions, mistrust, irritability, distance, and in how you treat people who had nothing to do with the original wound.

Many marriages, friendships, and families suffer, not only

because of current issues, but because of old wounds that were never named. Past hurt becomes a lens. You begin to hear with wounded ears and see with wounded eyes. Everyday moments feel heavier than they really are, because everything passes through the filter of what has not yet healed.

Different Faces of Wounding

Betrayal

Some wounds come from betrayal. Betrayal is one of the deepest relational pains because it comes from someone who had the power to remain loyal and chose not to. When loyalty breaks, something in the heart breaks in a different way.

You start to question others, but you also start to question yourself. Your worth, your discernment, your judgment, your significance all come under attack. The betrayal tries to speak louder than the truth of who you are. For a while, it even tries to become your identity.

Yet even betrayal, as devastating as it feels, can be healed when it is brought into the light of God's presence and truth.

Abandonment

Other wounds come from abandonment. Abandonment plants a fear that lingers long after the moment passes. You begin to expect people to leave. You prepare yourself for disappointment in advance. You stay guarded, careful, and on alert.

Even in healthy relationships, you struggle to rest in love because you fear it may vanish overnight. Abandonment trains the heart to be suspicious. But what abandonment breaks, God restores.

Deuteronomy 31:6 reminds me that He never leaves and never forsakes. There is no wound of abandonment so deep that His presence cannot fill it.

Dishonor

There are wounds that come from dishonor. Moments when someone belittles you, dismisses you, rejects your efforts, minimizes your pain, or makes you feel small and unworthy.

These wounds do not leave visible scars, but they bruise the heart. Dishonor attacks identity. It makes you want to shrink, silence your voice, or doubt your gifts. Still, your worth is not defined by how others treat you. God's affirmation carries more weight than human rejection.

The Wound of Silence

Then there are wounds caused by silence. Silence may seem like nothing, but it is something. When someone who should protect you does not. When someone who should speak up stays quiet. When someone who should apologize never does. Silence turns into its own kind of injury.

You are left longing for closure that never comes. Naming the wound means even acknowledging the things that were never said and the actions that never came.

Unintentional Wounds

Some wounds are never intended. A parent tries their best but does not know how to love well. A spouse fights battles you do not understand. A friend reacts out of their own brokenness.

Hurt does not always come from evil motives. Sometimes it comes from human weakness. But the impact is still real. Naming the wound does not mean you accuse, judge, or condemn. It simply means you allow the truth to be seen. And truth is always the starting point for healing.

Meeting God in the Truth

The beauty of God is that He meets you where you really are, not where you pretend to be. He does not heal masks. He heals hearts. He does not heal illusions. He heals reality. He does not heal what you hide. He heals what you bring to Him.

So naming your wound becomes an act of faith. It is your way of saying to God that this is where it hurts, trusting that the One who sees you will not turn away.

When Jesus Asks You What You Want

In Mark 10, Jesus meets a blind man named Bartimaeus. Bartimaeus cries out for mercy, and Jesus asks him what he wants Him to do. From the outside, this question seems unnecessary. Everyone can see that the man is blind. Yet Jesus does not assume. He invites Bartimaeus to say what he needs. Healing starts when he names what is wrong.

In that moment, Jesus is not asking for information. He is inviting participation. The same happens with you. God already knows your wound. He knows every detail. But healing involves your voice. You need to say what you want Him to heal.

The Power of Naming What Hurt You

There is power in naming what hurt you. When you do, the

wound starts to lose some of its grip. Hidden pain multiplies in the dark. Exposed pain begins to shrink in the light.

When you name the wound, you move it out of the shadows of your heart and into God's presence. And nothing that steps into His light stays the same. Darkness cannot remain where light is active.

Naming the wound does not mean you tear it open to bleed again. It means you allow God to touch it so it can finally close. You give language to your inner world so your heart can process what happened, instead of staying stuck in silent emotion.

You give yourself permission to feel, to remember, to reflect, and even to grieve. Grief is part of healing. You cannot forgive what you have not grieved. Grief is not weakness. It is the heart's way of releasing what cannot be changed.

Living With a Limp

Your wound may be fresh. It may be old. It may be something you carry for so long that you learn to function with it, like someone who learns to walk with a limp.

The limp becomes normal, but normal does not always mean healthy. God does not design you to walk through life with an emotional limp. His desire is wholeness.

Some people even build an identity around their hurt. Their personality shifts. Their voice changes. Their dreams shrink. Their behavior, reactions, and relationships all bend around the wound.

This does not happen because they want it. It happens

because the hurt was never named. Unacknowledged pain becomes a silent teacher, shaping how you love, trust, speak, react, and believe. It is impossible to move freely into the future while holding pain that keeps you rooted in the past.

Courage, Not Self-Pity

Naming your wound is not self-pity. It is courage. It is your heart saying that you are ready to heal. It is your past no longer allowed to control your future. It is the enemy no longer allowed to use what you keep in the dark. It is you reminding yourself that you are created to be whole.

Forgiveness always begins with truth. The truth is that you are hurt. Something is taken from you. Maybe peace. Maybe innocence. Maybe trust, confidence, safety, dignity, joy, or stability.

Naming the wound means identifying what was lost so that you can invite God to restore it. Joel 2:25 speaks of God restoring the years that the locust has eaten. God does not simply heal. He restores. He gives back more than what was taken.

Honesty and Mercy Working Together

Restoration does not begin until the wound is acknowledged. You cannot heal what you pretend does not hurt. You cannot forgive what you refuse to face. You cannot move forward while clinging to something God is gently asking you to release.

Healing is a partnership between your honesty and God's mercy. So before you move further on this journey of forgiveness, give your heart a moment to speak.

What hurt you? Who hurt you? What moment changed you?

What wound did you bury because you did not know what else to do with it? Do not rush this. Healing is not a race. It is a process. Every process starts with a first step.

This Is Where Healing Begins

As you read, you may feel emotions rising. Tears, memories, anger, confusion, or even numbness. All of these are part of naming the wound. You may feel the urge to shut down and protect yourself again. But remember, you are not revisiting the wound to live in it. You are revisiting it so God can finally heal it.

When love hurts, the heart learns to fear. God's love teaches the heart to heal. Human love may have wounded you, but divine love heals you. And that healing begins here, in this moment, with one simple truth: you are hurt, and God cares deeply about it.

As we walk this journey together, understand that naming your wound is not weakness. It is the doorway to strength. It is the point where healing begins. It is the moment your heart steps out of hiding and into God's hands.

And in His hands, every wound can heal. This is your road to forgiveness. Step by step. Truth by truth. Grace by grace. And it begins with this simple, life-changing act: naming your wound.

Chapter 2: The Weight Of Not Forgiving

Unforgiveness is one of the heaviest burdens a human heart can carry. It does not always announce itself loudly, yet it settles quietly into the soul, takes up space, shapes emotions, and influences how you react long after the original hurt passes. If hurt is the wound, unforgiveness is like the infection that sets in when the wound is left unattended, and over time it begins to change how you see yourself, how you see others, and even how you see God.

Why Unforgiveness Feels So Justified

The difficult thing about unforgiveness is that it often feels right. When someone hurts you deeply, there is a part of you that believes holding on to anger or pain keeps you safe, and you tell yourself that forgiving is too soft, that it excuses what happened, or that it somehow rewards the one who hurt you. These thoughts feel noble in the moment, but they are rooted in a lie, because unforgiveness never truly protects you, it only traps you. It builds walls so high and so thick that even the comfort God offers feels far away, not because He moves from you, but because your heart becomes guarded in all the wrong ways.

One of the sobering truths about unforgiveness is that it feels righteous, yet it does not produce anything righteous inside you. It feels powerful, yet it quietly drains your strength. It feels like control, yet it creates bondage. It feels like justice, yet it denies you the healing your heart needs. Pain tells you that holding on will keep you safe, but God gently shows that holding on keeps the wound open, and this is why unforgiveness becomes a silent enemy that keeps hearts captive, relationships strained, and souls distant from the fullness God wants you to experience.

How Unforgiveness Begins to Show

Many people do not notice when unforgiveness first begins to appear. It rarely starts with loud outbursts or obvious rage, it usually begins as a small discomfort, a shift in how you feel when a certain name is mentioned, or a quiet tension around certain places or memories. It hides in sarcasm, in long silences, in avoiding calls or visits, and in being overly cautious with your heart. You can be smiling on the outside but carrying a storm on the inside, and you can be functioning in your daily responsibilities while limping emotionally and feeling drained. You can even be active in ministry, serving faithfully, yet still be exhausted inside, because unforgiveness does not ask for permission, it moves in when pain is left unprocessed.

Unforgiveness is like drinking poison slowly while hoping the other person suffers from it. This picture is uncomfortable, yet it explains what really happens when you hold on to offense, because refusing to forgive does not damage the person who hurt you as much as it damages you. It begins to touch your peace, your joy, your thoughts, your sleep, your body, and your relationships with people who did nothing to you. Even natural studies show that emotional burdens can create physical symptoms like headaches, tension, lack of sleep, tiredness, or anxiety that never seems to end, and long before research confirms this, Proverbs 17 verse 22 already describes how a broken spirit dries up the bones and how pain that is not released slowly turns inward.

The Spiritual Cost of Holding On

Unforgiveness does not only affect your emotions and your body, it also contaminates your spiritual life. It is impossible to hold bitterness tightly in one hand and fully receive the life of God in the other hand at the same time, because bitterness blocks blessings and makes your heart heavy and dull. It clouds your discernment, makes you less sensitive to the Holy Spirit, and causes spiritual things to feel harder than they need to be.

Jesus speaks clearly about forgiveness, not to place a religious rule on you, but to protect your heart from what unforgiveness does. In Matthew 6 verse 15 He teaches that if you refuse to forgive others, you step outside of the flow of the forgiveness you yourself need, and this is not a threat, it is a spiritual principle. You cannot deeply receive what you stubbornly refuse to give, and a heart that stays closed toward people slowly begins to close toward God as well.

When you hold on to unforgiveness, something in your heart starts to harden. At first it is small and hardly noticeable, but over time you become less patient, less trusting, less hopeful, and less joyful. You start to interpret neutral actions as threats, ordinary comments as attacks, and normal disappointments as betrayals, and suddenly you find yourself expecting the worst, not because everyone is dangerous, but because your wound has become the lens through which you see. You begin to assume motives, imagine dangers that are not there, and guard yourself from possibilities that never actually existed, and this is the quiet work unforgiveness does when it is not dealt with.

Avoidance, Hiding, and Closed Hearts

Sometimes unforgiveness shows itself through avoidance. You find yourself avoiding certain people, places, conversations, or special days that remind you of what happened, and you avoid vulnerability because you are afraid of being hurt again. You avoid deep relationships and settle for surface-level connections because independence feels safer, yet avoiding does not heal anything, it only hides it. Anything you hide remains untouched, and what remains untouched cannot be healed. God works deeply in hearts that stay open, but unforgiveness tries to convince you to close everything and protect yourself at all times.

Unforgiveness acts like a spiritual parasite. It attaches itself to your heart and slowly feeds on your emotions until your joy becomes weak, your strength feels low, and your peace is drained. Instead of responding with wisdom, you react out of pain. Instead of healthy discernment, you become suspicious. Instead of feeling secure, you live defensive. Over time, unforgiveness begins to affect how you treat people who never hurt you, and this is one of the cruelest effects of holding on to offense, because you end up hurting the innocent out of wounds that came from the guilty.

When Old Hurt Enters New Relationships

Many marriages and close relationships suffer, not only because of present conflict, but because of old wounds that are never addressed. A husband or wife can carry hurt from childhood, former relationships, broken promises, or deep disappointments, and without realizing it, bring all that unhealed pain into the marriage. Pain that is not healed builds layers around the heart, and each layer creates more distance between people who truly love each other. As the heart hardens, affection feels complicated, trust becomes fragile, and communication becomes tense and defensive. This is why forgiveness is not only for the past, it is also protection for your present relationships, because you need to forgive those who hurt you so that you do not bleed on those who love you.

Hebrews 12 verse 15 gives a strong warning about a root of bitterness that grows and causes trouble and defiles many. Bitterness does not stay in one corner of your life, if it takes root, it spreads into your words, your thoughts, your moods, your choices, your prayers, and even your sense of calling. It begins small and hidden, like a root under the ground, and it is prevented by paying attention to your heart and choosing forgiveness early rather than waiting until resentment grows into a forest.

Lies Unforgiveness Tells

Unforgiveness whispers lies to the heart in very convincing ways. It tries to tell you that forgiving means forgetting, when in reality forgiveness allows you to remember without reliving the pain in the same way. It tells you that forgiving means you must trust again immediately, when trust and forgiveness are not the same and do not move at the same speed. It suggests that forgiving always leads to reconciliation, when sometimes wisdom and safety mean that reconciliation is not possible or not wise right now. Unforgiveness convinces you that letting go means you lose, but in God's design, letting go is exactly how you win back your peace and your life.

The enemy uses unforgiveness very strategically. He knows that he does not always need to attack your body if he can poison your heart. He celebrates division, distance, and broken connection, and he is pleased when families are fractured, when friendships die, when people isolate, and when love grows cold. John 10 verse 10 reminds me that the thief comes to steal, kill, and destroy, and one of the easiest ways he does this is by convincing you that holding on to pain is a sign of strength. True strength is not in holding the pain tightly, true strength is in releasing it into God's hands.

Carrying What Should Be Buried

Unforgiveness can feel like walking through life while carrying a corpse on your back. The event may be long over, the moment may have passed years ago, and the person who caused the hurt may have moved on, yet you still carry the weight of what happened as if it is happening today. Every day you relive a moment that no longer exists. Every day you drag a weight that cannot change. Every day you suffer under a memory that has more authority over you than it should. Forgiveness cuts the rope between you and what wounded you, and it speaks to your past and says that it will not own you anymore, and it speaks to the enemy and announces that the battle over this area of your heart ends now.

One of the most damaging effects of unforgiveness is the way it tries to rewrite your identity. You start to see yourself through what someone did rather than through what God says. If someone betrays you, you begin to feel worthless. If someone abandons you, you begin to feel unlovable. If someone mistreats you, you begin to feel inadequate. If someone constantly silences you, you begin to feel as if your voice carries no value. Unforgiveness ties your identity to another person's actions, but forgiveness returns your identity to the truth of who God says you are.

God Who Heals the Heart

Scripture shows the heart of God toward your pain in many places. In Exodus 15 verse 26 God reveals Himself as Jehovah Rapha, the Lord who heals you, which means healing is part of His nature, not a reluctant act. He does not only want to mend physical bodies, He desires to heal the broken parts of your heart, the parts that have been silenced, shamed, or shattered by what you went through. The healing He offers requires that you release what is poisoning you inside, and that release is what forgiveness starts to do.

Unforgiveness is deceptive because it often hides behind a busy life. Many people throw themselves into work, ministry, achievements, and constant activity because they hope that success or busyness will numb the pain in their hearts. Yet productivity is not the same as healing, and you can be publicly successful and privately broken at the same time. You can be gifted and still wounded, you can preach and still hurt, you can smile and still bleed inside, and healing does not come from doing more but from surrendering more to God.

Isolation and Distance from the Holy Spirit

Unforgiveness also pushes you toward isolation. You convince yourself that you are simply protecting your heart, but what you are really doing is cutting yourself off from love, comfort, and support at the very moment you need them most. Love thrives where there is openness and honesty, but unforgiveness demands secrecy and withdrawal, and it pressures you to keep everything bottled up and trust nobody. Isolation feels like safety for a while, but it is actually emotional and spiritual starvation, because your heart is created to receive love, comfort, truth, and healthy connection, and unforgiveness keeps those gifts far away.

When you cling to unforgiveness, you also create distance between your heart and the gentle leading of the Holy Spirit. He speaks with a soft voice, but unforgiveness makes so much noise inside that His whisper becomes harder to hear. He offers comfort, but unforgiveness keeps you restless. He brings clarity, but unforgiveness clouds your inner vision. Forgiveness, on the other hand, clears space in your heart, quiets the inner noise, and makes room again for God's voice to be heard and followed.

Do They Deserve It

Some people find it very hard to forgive because they feel strongly that the person who hurt them does not deserve forgiveness, and in some situations that may be true. The person may not deserve it from a human point of view, and they may not even be sorry. But forgiveness is never based on what they deserve, it is based on what you need. You need freedom, you need peace, you need the ability to move forward without heaviness chained to your back. Forgiveness is not a gift to the offender first, it is a gift to the one who is wounded.

Others struggle to forgive because they are afraid that if they let go, the pain will return or they will feel exposed again. The truth is that holding on to unforgiveness does not prevent pain, it stretches it out and keeps it alive. Pain begins to heal when it is surrendered into God's care, and you cannot truly heal while you cling tightly to the very thing that keeps cutting you. Forgiveness is not denial, it does not pretend that nothing happened, and it does not shrink the seriousness of what you went through. Forgiveness simply releases your right to hold on to it and hands that right over to God.

What Forgiveness Is and Is Not

Forgiveness does not restore trust in an instant, because trust takes time, rebuilding, honest change, and wisdom. Forgiveness does not automatically rebuild relationship, because relationship involves two willing hearts, while forgiveness can happen in one heart alone. Forgiveness does not force you back into unsafe spaces or unhealthy patterns, it allows you to walk free from emotional debt while still using discernment to protect yourself from further harm.

To forgive is not to say that it did not matter, to forgive is to say that it mattered deeply, but it will not control you anymore. Forgiveness is the decision to release the weight that has been crushing your heart and to refuse to stay bound when God is inviting you into freedom. It is obedience to God, but it is also compassion toward your own heart, because you recognize that you are not created to carry that level of pain forever.

The Weight and the Freedom

As this journey continues, one truth must stay clear in your heart, you cannot walk the road of forgiveness while clinging to the weight of unforgiveness. The weight needs to be noticed, understood, and then released into God's hands. God is not asking you to carry what He is willing to lift, and the same God who calls you to forgive also gives you the strength to forgive. The same God who asks for your burden also offers His peace in return.

The weight of unforgiveness is real, and you may feel it in your mind, your body, and your relationships, but the freedom that forgiveness brings is just as real and even greater. The freedom waiting in front of you is far more valuable than the pain that sits behind you, and as you release unforgiveness step by step, you begin to experience that freedom in ways you may not even have imagined yet.

Chapter 3: Perceptions That Block Healing

P erception Perception is a powerful force in your life. It shapes what you believe, how you respond, and how you interpret the world around you. Two people can walk through the same moment and still carry completely different stories about what happened, simply because they see it differently. In relationships, perception can strengthen the bond between two people or slowly create distance. In your healing journey, perception can either lead your heart toward forgiveness or keep it caught in cycles of hurt.

When Pain Changes How You See

When pain enters the heart, your perception often shifts without you even noticing. What once feels simple now feels complicated, what once feels clear becomes confusing, and what once feels light starts to feel very heavy. Pain quietly distorts perception and makes you see life through the lens of the wound instead of the lens of truth. Unforgiveness creates a kind of spiritual cataract in the heart, an inner blur that makes you misread even good intentions, and soon you realize that nothing looks the same when you look at it through a wounded heart.

Forgiveness Is Not Excusing

One of the most damaging perceptions people carry is the idea that forgiving someone means excusing what they have done. This misunderstanding keeps many hearts from healing. Forgiveness does not excuse the offence, it brings it into God's presence. It does not minimize the pain, it actually acknowledges it fully. It does not turn what was wrong into something right, it simply refuses to let that wrong keep ruling your life. When you choose to forgive, you are not erasing the truth of what happened, you are removing the sting that keeps you tied to that memory.

Forgiveness and Reconciliation Are Not the Same

Another perception that needs to shift early is the idea that forgiveness always means reconciliation. Reconciliation is a journey that involves two people. Forgiveness is a decision that starts in one heart. You can forgive someone completely and still not return to the relationship in the same way, and sometimes it is wise, healthy, or even necessary to keep a distance. In some stories reconciliation is possible and beautiful, in others it is unsafe, unwise, or simply not possible. Your healing does not depend on whether the relationship is restored, because your healing is a matter between you and God, and the condition of your heart does not have to follow the condition of that relationship.

Forgiving Does Not Mean Forgetting

Many people also believe that forgiveness requires forgetting. That little phrase about forgiving and forgetting has created confusion for years. Forgetting is not what God asks of you. He does not ask you to wipe your memory clean, He asks you to allow Him to transform it. Forgetting is not healing, because if you forget completely, you cannot learn, you cannot testify, and you cannot grow wiser. True healing is when you remember without reliving, when you can look back at a painful memory and it no longer controls your emotions, your reactions, or your identity in the way it once did.

Time Alone Does Not Heal

Pain often creates the perception that time alone will heal the wound. You tell yourself that if you just wait long enough, it will stop hurting. Time can create distance, but distance is not the same as healing. Time can make you numb, but numbness is not restoration. Time can help you function, but functioning is not freedom. Deep healing does not come from time passing, it comes from truth entering. It comes from surrender, from acknowledging the wound, placing it in God's hands, and allowing His Spirit to do what time by itself cannot do. Time may move the calendar forward, but only God truly moves the heart forward.

Forgiveness, Trust, and Boundaries

There is also the perception that forgiving someone means allowing them back into your life in the same way as before. This is not true. Forgiveness is something that happens in a moment of decision, trust is something that is rebuilt over time. Trust grows through consistent behavior, honesty, and change. Trust is wisdom in action, while forgiveness is grace in action. You can forgive someone completely and still protect your heart with healthy boundaries. You are not called to repeatedly place yourself in the same kind of harm and call it forgiveness, because that is not forgiveness, that is neglecting your own wellbeing. Forgiveness frees your heart, and wisdom guards it.

Suppression Is Not Forgiveness

Some people believe that forgiving means they must suppress their feelings. They think they have to smile when they want to cry, serve when they feel empty, or embrace when they are still hurting inside. Suppression is not forgiveness, it is emotional avoidance that often hides behind spiritual language. God does not invite you to pretend, He invites you to be honest. He welcomes your tears, your anger, your confusion, and your disappointment. Forgiveness is not the absence of feeling, it is bringing those feelings to God and allowing Him to hold them, heal them, and shape them.

Waiting for an Apology

Another perception that keeps hearts stuck is the belief that the offender must apologize first. While an apology can be meaningful and bring closure, it is not a requirement for forgiveness. Not everyone will apologize. Some people do not realize the depth of the pain they have caused. Some are too proud to admit it. Some are no longer alive to say they are sorry. If your healing depends on another person's action, you give them control over your future. Forgiveness removes that control. Forgiveness releases you from waiting for something that may never happen and allows you to move forward anyway.

Strength Is in Letting Go

Pain can also convince you that holding on to the hurt makes you strong. You see forgiveness as weakness, as surrender, as losing the fight, but the opposite is true. Forgiveness is a sign of strength, courage, and spiritual maturity. Anyone can carry a grudge, that takes no skill at all. It takes real strength to release it. Anyone can repay hurt with hurt, it takes grace to choose a higher way. Jesus forgives while hanging on the cross, and that is not weakness, that is authority, that is power, that is love in its purest form. When you forgive, you walk in that same kind of spiritual authority, even if your situation looks very different.

Forgiveness, Vulnerability, and Wisdom

Many people are afraid that if they forgive, they will automatically become vulnerable again and be open to more hurt. Vulnerability feels risky when your heart has already been wounded. Forgiveness does not force you into vulnerability. Forgiveness frees you on the inside so that you do not live with emotional chains wrapped around your heart. Vulnerability is a choice you make with wisdom and discernment, forgiveness is a command that God gives for your good. Forgiveness opens your heart, wisdom protects it, love restores it, and healing strengthens it for what comes next.

Forgiveness and Justice

There is another perception that often stands in the way, the belief that forgiveness erases justice. Many people stay angry because they feel their anger is the only way they can keep a sense of justice alive. They fear that if they let go, it will feel like the offender has escaped accountability. Forgiveness does not cancel justice, it simply transfers justice from your hands to God's hands. Romans 12 verse 19 reminds you that vengeance belongs to the Lord, not to you. When you forgive, you are not abandoning justice, you are trusting it to the One who sees everything clearly, judges rightly, and restores in ways you cannot.

Where Was God

Pain can also whisper that God was absent when the wound entered your life. This is a deeply painful perception, and many hearts quietly ask where God was, why He did not stop it, and why He did not protect them. The truth is that God's presence is not proven by the absence of pain, it is seen in His nearness in the middle of pain.

God does not always prevent brokenness in this world, but He does promise to redeem it. He does not always stop every storm, but He walks with you through it. He does not always remove every thorn, but He provides grace that is enough for it. Healing begins to move in your heart when you realize that God did not abandon you, He is the One carrying you toward restoration even when you do not feel it.

Unforgiveness Does Not Punish Them

Another perception that keeps hearts bound is the belief that unforgiveness punishes the offender. You may think that if you forgive, it will feel like they got away with what they did. The truth is that unforgiveness does not punish the offender, it punishes you. It steals your sleep, your peace, your joy, and your hope. It ties you to a moment that no longer exists and binds you to a memory that cannot change. When you forgive, you are not letting them off the hook, you are removing the hook from your own heart.

When Pain Writes the Story

Pain also creates assumptions, and those assumptions shape how you see everything. You start to assume motives, assume intentions, and assume thoughts that may not reflect the true story. Perception shapes the story you tell yourself, and that story shapes how you react. You can start to see danger where there is none, betrayal where there is simple misunderstanding, and rejection where there is only distance or difference. Healing requires that you are willing to question the stories your pain is telling you. Not everything your pain whispers is true, and part of healing is learning to separate the story from the wound so that your heart can receive truth instead of assumption.

Fences Around the Heart

Holding on to pain often feels like a form of protection. It is like building a fence around your heart and telling yourself that if nobody gets too close, nobody can hurt you again. The problem is that fences do not only keep danger out, they keep healing out as well. You cannot live a life of love from behind walls of fear. God designs your heart to be guarded with wisdom, not imprisoned by fear. Forgiveness does not erase your boundaries, it erases your fear of being ruled by pain. When your heart heals, your boundaries become healthy and protective instead of cold and defensive.

Healing Is Not Passive

One of the most subtle perceptions is the belief that healing is passive. Some people think that if God wants to heal them, He will do it without their involvement. Healing is a gift from God, but it is not a passive experience. When Jesus speaks to the man at the pool of Bethesda and tells him to pick up his mat and walk, He is not ignoring the man's pain, He is inviting him to participate in his own healing. Healing is active and intentional. It asks you to reflect, to surrender, to pray, to face truth, and to work through emotions instead of running from them. It takes courage to say to God that this is your pain and you are placing it in His hands, and healing comes as you surrender, not just as you wait.

Forgiveness as a Process

There is also the perception that forgiveness must happen all at once and never be revisited. In reality, forgiveness is both a moment and a journey. It starts with a decision you make before God, but it often continues with daily choices to surrender the hurt again when it rises. There will be days when the pain feels strong again and the memory tries to speak loudly. These moments do not mean you have failed in forgiving, they simply mean you are human and still healing. Healing is rarely a straight line, it is layered and gradual, and each layer you surrender brings you closer to real freedom.

Letting Truth Reshape Your Perception

To walk the road of forgiveness, you need to confront the perceptions that keep your heart tied up. You need to let truth replace assumption, wisdom replace fear, grace replace anger, and God's perspective replace the one shaped only by pain. Your perception may have been formed in seasons of deep hurt, but it does not have to define the rest of your life. Healing begins when you surrender your perception to God's truth. Freedom begins when the lies your pain taught you are replaced with what God says. Forgiveness begins when your heart chooses truth over what feels familiar. The road ahead may not always feel easy, but it is a beautiful road, and as your perception shifts, your healing will deepen and your heart will begin to breathe freely again.

Chapter 4: Facing The Truth: What Actually Happened

Truth is often the hardest companion on the road to forgiveness. It asks for honesty and vulnerability. It asks us to stop running, not from other people, but from ourselves. Still, truth is also what starts loosening the knots in the heart. It makes healing possible. It brings hidden memories into the open and places them in God's hands.

For many people, healing feels far away because truth feels risky. Instead of facing it, they spend years avoiding it. Sometimes they do it on purpose, and sometimes they do not even realize they are doing it. They fear what might rise to the surface if they let themselves see clearly. Pain can be blinding like that. It can make us rewrite the story so it hurts less, so we feel protected, or so we stay justified in our anger. But truth is not here to shame us. Truth is here to set us free.

A lot of people get stuck on the day they were hurt. Life moves on, routines change, and years pass, but the heart stays in that one moment. That moment starts shaping reactions, feeding fear, and coloring relationships. When the heart is frozen there, truth gets cloudy. Healing asks us to let that moment thaw, so we can see what really happened, not just what pain keeps repeating.

Truth Helps Us Look Back Without Living Back There

Looking back is uncomfortable. The past can feel like a room we never want to walk into again. It holds memories we tried to bury, conversations we wish we could erase, faces we stopped looking at, and versions of ourselves we barely recognize. So it makes sense that we avoid truth, because we think looking back means reliving everything.

But healing is not about moving backward. It is about bringing the past into God's presence so it loses its grip on the present. Looking back is not reopening a wound for no reason. It is exposing what is infected, so it can actually heal. God does not heal what we hide. He heals what we bring into His light. Scripture reminds us that God already knows what is buried inside us, even the parts we cannot put into words. Facing the truth is not about informing God. It is about letting God reshape the way our hearts understand the story.

Pain Talks First, but Truth Speaks Last

Pain usually grabs the microphone before anything else. It is loud, emotional, and impulsive. It tells stories that feel real but are not always accurate. It says the wound defines you. It says the person who hurt you still has power over you. It says nobody understands, nobody cares, and nobody can be trusted again. Pain wants to write the final chapter.

Truth interrupts that. Truth says the wound shaped you, but it does not define you. Truth says the person who hurt you cannot keep you captive forever. Truth says God sees everything and stays present even in the moments that shatter you. Truth says your future is not tied to the person who broke your heart. When truth comes in, it quietly corrects the lies pain has repeated for years. Without truth, we carry emotional illusions. With truth, we carry clarity.

Holding on to pain can feel like power, like proof that what happened matters. But really it is like hugging a cactus and expecting the other person to feel the thorns. Truth helps us admit that holding on does not protect us, it keeps piercing us. That honesty hurts, but it also opens the door.

Truth Helps Us See People Clearly

Facing truth means seeing ourselves clearly, and it also means seeing the person who hurt us clearly. That part can feel almost impossible. Pain loves to paint the offender as a monster who acted only out of cruelty. Sometimes that is true. But sometimes people act out of their own brokenness, immaturity, fear, ignorance, or unresolved pain. Some hurt us on purpose. Some hurt us without realizing what they are doing. Some hurt us because they are hurting too.

None of that excuses what they did. None of it makes the wound smaller or the pain less valid. Still, seeing others clearly helps separate what they did from who they are. It reminds us that people are complex and flawed, and that their actions often come from unhealed places. Understanding does not erase the damage. It just removes unnecessary hatred. It helps the heart soften toward healing, even if trust is not restored.

Truth Helps Us Name What We Lost

Forgiveness gets harder when we only focus on what was done to us instead of what was taken from us. We cannot release what we cannot name. Facing truth means identifying the specific losses attached to the hurt.

For some people the loss is trust. For others it is safety,

dignity, innocence, security, identity, or even years of peace that never came back the same. Naming what we lost matters because it gives language to grief. It lets the heart feel what it has been carrying. It also lets God meet us in specific places, not vague ones. We cannot heal a wound we refuse to look at, and we cannot forgive a pain we refuse to name. Truth asks us to sit with the memory long enough to understand what really broke.

Truth Shows Us Our Reactions Honestly

Truth also asks us to notice what the wound does to us over time. Hurt changes behavior long after the moment of offense. We may grow guarded, colder, more suspicious, or emotionally distant. We may expect pain where there is none. We may start reading love as danger, affection as manipulation, and honesty as an attack.

Truth is not pointing this out to shame us. It is pointing it out to free us. When we see how pain reshapes us, we can start reclaiming what was lost, or even discovering who we are becoming in God. Anger held too long can turn into a habit, and habits can become a kind of character. That is why truth asks a hard but healing question: What have I become since the hurt? Not so we can condemn ourselves, but so we can recover the parts of the heart pain has muted.

Truth Helps Us See God Clearly Again

Truth is not only about the wound and the offender. It is also about God. Pain can distort how we see Him. Deep down some people believe that if God truly loved them, He would have prevented the hurt. They sit with the quiet question of where God was when it happened.

Facing truth means letting God define Himself in the middle of our pain. He is present. He sees. He understands. He cares. He does not leave. God's presence is not proven by a life without pain. It is proven by His power to redeem pain. The cross shows us that God takes the worst suffering and turns it into the doorway for love, restoration, and healing. That same truth applies here. Your wound is not permanent, and God is not distant. He is closest to the brokenhearted.

Truth Takes Courage

Truth does not always feel gentle. It comes with weight and clarity, and it asks for courage. It invites you into the parts of your story you tried to bury. It asks you to speak honestly without editing, pretending, or shrinking what happened.

Courage does not mean you feel strong. Courage means you choose to face what hurts even if your voice is shaking. It means trusting that God will not drown you in memories, but will use those memories to lift you into healing.

Truth Is the First Door to Forgiveness

We cannot walk the road to forgiveness without stepping through truth first. We cannot release what we have not faced. We cannot surrender what we have not acknowledged. Truth makes forgiveness possible, not because it erases pain, but because it shows the way forward.

Truth does not change the past, but it changes our relationship with the past. It removes poison from the wound. It does not make the offender right. It makes your heart free. Truth is not for them. It is for you.

Healing depends on a willingness to see clearly. Freedom grows where honesty lives. Restoration begins when we face what is real. And here is what is real: you are hurt, but you are not beyond healing. You are wounded, but God restores. You are broken, but nothing God touches stays broken. Your truth is not your end. It is your beginning, and from that beginning forgiveness becomes possible.

Chapter 5: How Pain Shapes The Heart

P Pain has a way of quietly shaping the heart. It does not just wound you, it starts molding you. It does not only break things, it reshapes how you move through life. Even when we do not want it to, pain forms new patterns in us, new fears, new habits, and new emotional reflexes. Every hurt carries a kind of power, the power to change us. Sometimes that change passes with time, but sometimes it sinks so deep that it starts steering the direction of our lives.

People often underestimate how much pain affects them. They think that once enough time goes by, the wound fades and they go back to who they were before. But pain leaves fingerprints on the soul. It touches places we did not know were vulnerable, and it wakes up emotions we did not know were sitting there. You might not notice the shift right away, but over time you realize something inside you feels different. You respond differently. You think differently. You protect yourself differently.

When hurt stays unresolved, it does not stay neutral. It slowly turns into a habit, and habits start looking like character. That is one of the sobering truths about pain. If it is not healed, it starts defining you. It becomes the lens you use to look at life, relationships, and even God.

When we do not confront pain, we start living from it. When

we do not heal pain, we start speaking from it. When we do not surrender pain, we start identifying with it. And the tricky part is, we often do not see how much it has shaped us until someone else points it out.

When Pain Becomes a Lens

A wounded heart rarely sees the world the same way again. Pain becomes a filter over everything. What should have been one moment in time starts replaying itself in the background, and then it colors every new moment with the shades of the old one. A simple comment feels like an attack. An honest mistake feels like betrayal. A small silence feels like rejection. A delayed text feels like proof that people cannot be trusted. Before long, the wound is talking louder than the truth.

This is where that subtle paranoia comes in. Not the dramatic kind, but the quiet emotional kind. The kind where you expect people to hurt you before they ever try to love you. The kind where your heart braces for pain even when none is present. The kind where you start preparing for abandonment because abandonment once cut you deep.

Pain that is not healed tries to protect itself, but it does it in unhealthy ways. It convinces you that caution is wisdom when it is really fear. It convinces you that detachment is maturity when it is really self-defense. It convinces you that isolation is strength when it is really survival. Pain trains the heart to live on guard.

When Pain Creates Emotional Reflexes

Pain does not only shape how you see. It shapes how you react. When a wound is left alone too long, emotions start responding from memory instead of reality. That is why people overreact to situations that do not call for that level of intensity. The heart remembers what it went through, and it answers the present with the force of the past.

A raised voice triggers old battles. A disagreement triggers insecurity. A simple question triggers shame. A pause in conversation triggers panic. A correction triggers feelings of inadequacy. The heart gets conditioned to respond from the wound instead of from the truth.

This is why forgiveness matters so much. It is not only about what someone else did. It is also about reclaiming your emotional world from what happened back then. Without forgiveness, emotions stay trapped in moments that no longer exist. You end up living in the past while trying to act like you are fully in the present.

Holding on to pain can change even the gentlest person into someone they barely recognize. Emotional wounds do not only come for your joy, they come for your identity. Pain can turn someone kind into someone cold. It can turn someone trusting into someone suspicious. It can turn someone loving into someone distant. Over time, you start losing parts of yourself that were never meant to die.

When Pain Silences the Heart

There is pain that makes you loud, and there is pain that makes you quiet. The loud kind shows up as anger, tears, frustration, or conflict. The quiet kind sinks deep and creates numbness. You stop expressing yourself. You stop asking for help. You stop trying to be understood because you believe your pain is too heavy, too inconvenient, or always misunderstood.

Silent pain is dangerous because it keeps telling you that you are fine. It says this is just life. It whispers that everyone hurts, so you will adjust. It insists that you should not bother anyone and should deal with it alone. This is how people smile while bleeding inside, function while exhausted, serve while empty, and look strong while falling apart on the inside.

Pain can quiet the heart, but silence is not meant to be your healing strategy. Healing needs honesty. Healing needs expression. Healing needs a voice. Silent pain is still pain, and if it stays unaddressed, it eventually grows into bitterness.

When Pain Breeds Bitterness

Bitterness is often the last stage of pain that stays unattended. It does not show up overnight. It grows quietly. It starts as anger, then becomes resentment, and then hardens into something heavier. Scripture warns about bitterness because God knows how destructive it is. It spreads. It defiles. It damages more than one heart.

Bitterness poisons marriages. It fractures friendships. It destroys families. It pulls children away from parents. It ruins community. And most painfully, it distances the heart from God. Unforgiveness reshapes a person. It distorts kindness, drains joy, replaces peace with tension, and turns love into suspicion. A bitter heart stops seeing good in people and good in moments, and sometimes it even struggles to see good in God. And the hard truth is that bitterness hurts the person carrying it far more than the person who caused it.

When Pain Turns Inward

Some pain turns outward and blames others. But some pain turns inward and blames you. This is the kind of pain that whispers self-hate. It tells you the hurt was your fault. It suggests you are the problem, that you deserved what happened, or that your value was never real to begin with. This internal pain is subtle, but it is deadly. It convinces you to stay small. It convinces you to stop hoping. It convinces you to settle for less. It convinces you to survive instead of live on purpose.

Refusing to forgive can quietly turn into self-punishment. When you hold on to pain, you can end up holding on to the belief that you deserved it. That is not the voice of God. That is the voice of shame, and shame never heals a heart. God does not create you to carry self-blame. He creates you to live under the reality of His grace.

When Pain Steals Joy

One of the most heartbreaking effects of unhealed pain is how it steals joy. Joy is not the same as happiness. Happiness depends on circumstances. Joy runs deeper. It is spiritual, rooted in God, anchored in gratitude, and present even in the middle of storms. Pain tries to put out that God-given joy by filling the heart with heaviness.

You may laugh, but you feel the limit to it. You may smile, but it starts feeling rehearsed. You may worship, but something feels weighed down. You may love, but your love stays guarded. Pain steals the lightness of life. It steals excitement for the future. It steals freedom in relationships.

Unhealed pain does not stay in the past. It follows you into every new season. But God's healing does not just patch over what happened. He restores what pain tries to steal.

Pain Is Not Meant to Shape You Forever

It is true that pain changes us, but it is not meant to define us. God intends pain to refine us, not trap us. He uses pain as a teacher, not a captor. Pain may shape your reactions for a season, but God shapes your identity for a lifetime.

That is why forgiveness is powerful. Forgiveness breaks the mold pain tries to keep you in. It interrupts the cycle. It softens what pain hardens. It restores what pain distorts. It teaches the heart to respond from grace instead of trauma. It helps the soul breathe again and the mind think clearly again. Pain can shape the heart, but forgiveness reshapes it.

God Heals What Pain Shapes

Scripture tells us that God heals the brokenhearted and binds up their wounds. This is not just poetic comfort. It is a promise. God does not only heal the wound itself. He restores the places pain has reshaped. He softens bitterness, calms paranoia, breaks unhealthy emotional reflexes, renews joy, and leads the heart back into freedom.

Healing does not erase your story. It redeems it. Healing does not delete the memory. It purifies it. Healing does not change the past, but it changes the power the past has over you. What pain twists, God straightens. What pain hardens, God softens. What pain silences, God revives. What pain buries, God brings back to life. That is why forgiveness matters, not to pretend the pain never happened, but to undo the damage it tries to leave behind.

Chapter 6: Why Forgiveness Is God's Pathway To Freedom

F orgiveness is one of those divine mysteries that the human heart wrestles with. It is simple enough to understand, yet difficult enough to practice. It is commanded in scripture, yet resisted in emotion. It is freedom wrapped in a decision that often feels unjust. It is the key to healing, yet it is the very thing the wounded heart avoids. And because of this tension, forgiveness becomes the one thing many desire but struggle to surrender to.

When Jesus speaks about forgiveness, He never presents it as a suggestion, a negotiation, or a gentle invitation. He speaks about it with the same seriousness that He speaks about faith, prayer, or righteousness. In Matthew 6:14–15, He says, "If you forgive others their trespasses, your heavenly Father will also forgive you; but if you do not forgive others, neither will your Father forgive yours." These words are not meant to frighten us; they are meant to awaken us. Jesus knew that unforgiveness does not only break relationships between people, it breaks intimacy between the person and God.

Unforgiveness as a spiritual blockage, a barrier that interrupts the flow of God's forgiveness toward us. If we withhold forgiveness, we shut the very door through which God desires to pour His mercy into our hearts. This is why forgiveness is not optional for the believer; it is essential. It is one of the most powerful acts of obedience a Christian can offer God, because it requires the surrender of pride, the humility of spirit, and the willingness to trust God with justice.

Yet forgiveness is so often misunderstood. Many imagine it to be a feeling, a warm release, a sudden peace, a moment when emotions align with truth. But forgiveness is not a feeling; it is a decision. It is an act of the will before it is an act of the emotions. If forgiveness depended on feeling ready, very few people would ever forgive. Feelings may take time to heal, but forgiveness is a choice that opens the door for those feelings to follow.

Pain whispers that forgiveness must be earned. Hurt insists that forgiveness should wait for an apology. Pride declares that forgiveness makes us weak. But God's Word teaches something different. It shows us that forgiveness is an act of spiritual strength, the kind of strength that is only possible when we surrender our rights to God.

Once again, your earlier writing spoke this truth plainly: "Forgiveness begins simply with the confession of the mouth: 'I forgive you,' even if the recipient is not there to receive it." That is because forgiveness is a conversation with God before it is a conversation with anyone else. It is a release, not a reunion. It is an act of obedience that happens in the secret place of the heart, where God sees, understands, and honors every attempt to let go.

But why does God insist on forgiveness so strongly? Why does He make it a non-negotiable part of the believer's life? The answer lies in the nature of God Himself. Forgiveness is at the core of who God is Forgiveness is the heart of the gospel. Forgiveness is the reason Jesus came.

From Genesis to Revelation, the story of Scripture is a story of a God who forgives relentlessly, generously, and sacrificially. A God whose love is so deep that He sends His only Son to bear the sins of humanity so that forgiveness becomes available to all. If we claim to follow Him, then forgiveness becomes not only something we receive but something we reflect.

Forgiving is our way of imitating the One who forgave us first. Forgiving is our way of participating in His heart. Forgiving is our way of demonstrating His nature to the world. When we forgive, we look like Jesus. When we refuse to forgive, we look like the old version of ourselves, the version Jesus came to transform.

One of the most painful truths of life is that the people who hurt us often move on more quickly than we do. They may never apologize. They may never admit their wrong. They may never acknowledge the damage. And if our healing depends on their actions, we become prisoners to their choices.

You may never receive an apology. And even if you do, it may not be the apology you imagined. People have their own pride, wounds, limitations, and blind spots. Many do not understand the depth of the pain they caused. Some do not want to understand. Some cannot understand. Forgiveness cannot wait for apology; forgiveness must flow from obedience.

This is where the human heart often struggles. Something within us longs for justice, for acknowledgment, for accountability. Something in us wants the person who caused us pain to experience some measure of the pain we felt. This desire is not inherently sinful; it is human. It is the heart's longing for balance, fairness, and closure.

But God never asked us to play the role of judge. That position belongs to Him alone. When we forgive, we are not denying justice; we are transferring it. We are placing justice in the hands of the One who sees the whole picture, who measures with perfect scales, who heals with perfect wisdom, and who restores with perfect love.

Forgiveness is not you excusing them. Forgiveness is you trusting God. Forgiveness is you saying, "Lord, You can handle this better than I can."

The enemy understands the spiritual power of forgiveness, which is why he fights it so fiercely. Unforgiveness gives him legal access to our emotions. It gives him permission to torment our thoughts. It gives him a voice in our minds. It grants him influence over our relationships. He knows that a heart filled with unforgiveness cannot fully receive the joy, peace, and clarity God desires to give.

Unforgiveness poisons the heart, clouds the mind, and robs us of every good thing God wants us to enjoy. And most painfully, unforgiveness separates us from the presence of God because God cannot dwell comfortably where hatred, bitterness, and resentment are allowed to remain.

Forgiveness is God's pathway to freedom because forgiveness restores spiritual alignment. It clears the heart. It breaks emotional chains. It dismantles bitterness. It silences the enemy. It restores peace. It makes room for joy. It opens the door for healing. It frees the soul from bondage. Forgiveness is not just an act; it is a spiritual cleansing.

Forgiveness is also God's pathway to freedom because it allows the heart to love again. You were designed to love. You were designed to trust, to connect, to breathe freely in relationships. But unforgiveness suffocates love. It wraps the heart in layers of self-protection until even the purest forms of love struggle to reach you.

Pain creates walls, but forgiveness tears them down. Pain closes the heart, but forgiveness opens it gently. Pain dims hope, but forgiveness reignites it. Pain shrinks the soul, but forgiveness expands it once again.

Forgiveness also frees you from the false belief that you are responsible for what happened. Many people quietly carry self-blame. They ask themselves endless questions, "Why didn't I see it coming?" "Why wasn't I enough?" "Why did I let it happen?" These questions create emotional prisons. But forgiveness helps you see the truth: you are not responsible for the choices of others. You are responsible only for your healing, your freedom, and your obedience to God.

In your earlier writing, you shared something profound, "If I could not forgive, then God would not forgive me too." That realization changed everything. This same realization has brought countless believers to surrender their pain at the feet of Jesus. Not because their offenders deserved it, but because they themselves needed to be free.

Forgiveness is transformative because it shifts the focus from what was done to you to what God is doing in you. It shifts the story from victimhood to victory. It shifts the narrative from brokenness to restoration. Forgiveness is the moment where God begins rewriting your life in His voice rather than the voice of your pain.

Forgiveness does not erase history; it rewrites destiny.

Forgiveness does not change the past; it changes your future. Forgiveness does not undo the wound; it heals the heart.

This is why forgiveness is God's pathway to freedom. It sets you free, free from the memory, free from the bitterness, free from the fear, free from the anger, free from the resentment, and free from the version of yourself shaped by hurt rather than by grace.

You may not feel ready to forgive, but forgiveness is not a feeling. You may not feel strong enough to forgive, but forgiveness is not strength, it is surrender. You may not feel whole enough to forgive, but forgiveness is the pathway that leads to wholeness.

Forgiveness is your act of telling God, "I choose freedom over pain. I choose Your way over mine. I choose to let go so that You can restore me." And when you choose forgiveness, heaven moves. The heart softens. The soul breathes again. The weight lifts. And the journey toward full healing begins.

Chapter 7: Surrendering The Wound To God

S urrender is one of the hardest parts of walking with God. It asks you to place your most fragile places into His hands, even though you can't see Him. It asks you to loosen your grip on the thing that feels like control, which is often your pain. And yet surrender is also one of the most freeing choices you ever make, because it's the moment you stop carrying the weight alone.

Over time, many of us learn a quiet truth. Holding on to pain doesn't protect us, it traps us. We cling to hurt because it feels familiar. We hold on to anger because it feels justified. We keep bitterness close because it feels like armor. Somewhere in our hearts we think that if we keep the wound near, we keep power over the memory. But the heart isn't built to carry what only God can heal.

Holding on can feel like survival, like a way to stay in control. But most of the time it turns into emotional self-torture. It's like grabbing a cactus and refusing to let go. You hold it tight thinking you're proving something, but you're the one bleeding. Surrender is the choice to open your hands.

The Illusion of Control

Pain whispers a lie that sounds convincing in the middle of hurt. It tells you that anger is power. It tells you that if you let go, the other person wins. It tells you that forgiving means pretending it didn't matter. It tells you that surrender means losing the last bit of control you have.

But pain doesn't give power, it drains it. It weakens you. It consumes your energy. It steals the strength you need for living, loving, praying, and growing. Anger can feel strong at first. It feels like fire that keeps you alert, until you realize that fire is burning you from the inside out. Unhealed pain convinces you the flames are protecting you, when they're slowly eating away at your heart.

Surrender doesn't remove your authority. It restores it. When you place your wound in God's hands, you stop being ruled by the memory of what happened. You start being led by the One who heals.

The Weight You Are Not Meant to Carry

God never designs you to carry unforgiveness. The human heart isn't made to store bitterness, resentment, or revenge. Those things erode the soul, cloud judgment, and leave a heaviness that follows you everywhere, into your conversations, your decisions, your relationships, and even your sleep.

Jesus speaks directly to that weight. He invites the weary and burdened to come to Him for rest. That rest isn't the absence of pain. It's the surrender of pain. Rest comes when you put what you can't carry into the hands of the God who carries you.

Some people hold wounds for years because they think releasing them dishonors the pain. But holding on doesn't honor it, it keeps it alive. Surrender honors God because it acknowledges that

He is the healer.

Letting God See What You Don't Want to Feel

Surrender is deeply honest. It's not mainly about being open with people, it's about being open with God. It means admitting where it hurts, how much it hurts, and how powerless you feel to fix it on your own. That kind of honesty can feel terrifying, especially if you've learned to appear strong, stay composed, and never show weakness.

But God isn't moved by your composure. He's moved by your transparency. Even Jesus brings His sorrow openly to the Father in the garden. He doesn't hide the weight He feels. He shows that bringing pain to God isn't failure, it's faith. When you surrender your wound, you're inviting God into the most tender part of your heart. You're saying you trust Him with what you can't handle. And God doesn't mishandle what you entrust to Him.

Why Surrender Feels Scary

A lot of people fear surrender because they think it leaves them exposed. They worry that if they let go of anger, they become vulnerable again. They worry they'll forget how deeply they were hurt. They worry that releasing the wound means lowering their guard.

But surrender doesn't make you vulnerable to harm. It makes you vulnerable to healing. It lets God place His hands where the wound still bleeds. And healing isn't weakness, it's strength coming back to life.

Pain may feel like a shield, but it's a terrible one. It can keep people out, and it can also keep God out. Surrender pulls down the walls pain builds, and it makes room for love, clarity, and restoration to enter again.

The Exchange That Happens in Surrender

Surrender isn't just letting go. It's an exchange. It's where God takes the weight you can't carry and replaces it with peace. He trades bitterness for joy, sorrow for comfort, anger for rest, confusion for clarity. This exchange is what makes forgiveness possible.

You don't forgive by straining harder. You forgive through God's strength in you. Healing doesn't come from willpower alone, it comes from God stepping into the wound. Forgiveness grows out of surrender the same way fruit grows out of a healthy tree.

Without surrender, forgiveness feels impossible. With surrender, forgiveness becomes a real path forward. The heart can't serve two masters. It will cling to the wound or cling to God. Surrender is choosing the One who heals.

The Risk and the Reward

There's a moment in every believer's journey where surrender feels like a risk. It feels like stepping into the unknown. It feels like opening your hands and not knowing what happens next. But every risk taken toward God becomes a reward of grace.

Surrender may feel like losing at first, but it's the only way you win your heart back from the past. It may feel like giving up control, but you're really giving up torment. It may feel like lowering your guard, but you're lifting your soul.

Forgiveness isn't about pretending you feel ready. Surrender starts where feelings end. It's obedience before it is emotion. And that obedience creates space for the heart to heal.

God Honors What You Place in His Hands

Whatever you surrender to God becomes what He transforms. The wound you give Him becomes a place of restoration. The pain you release becomes the space where His glory meets you. The disappointment you loosen becomes the beginning of something new.

God asks Moses what is in his hand, and Moses is holding something ordinary. But once it is surrendered, God turns it into a tool for miracles. In the same way, your wound may feel too heavy to carry and too painful to touch, but once you surrender it, it becomes the place where God does deep healing work.

Forgiveness begins on the altar of surrender. Healing begins where pain is released. Freedom begins where wounds are placed in God's hands. You don't heal by tightening your grip. You heal by letting go. Surrender isn't the end of your story. It's the beginning of a new one, and God writes that story with tenderness, wisdom, and redemption.

Chapter 8: Understanding The Person: Not Excusing But Seeing Clearly

T here comes a moment in every healing journey when the heart runs into a truth it does not really want to face. The person who hurt you is still a person. Not a villain. Not a monster. Not some dark shadow. Just a human being with their own wounds, fears, weaknesses, blind spots, and broken places. That realization can feel unfair, especially when the pain is still fresh. Anger makes it feel like they deserve only judgment. But as healing starts doing its work, something softer begins to grow in you. It does not erase what happened, and it does not pretend the wound is small, but it invites you to see the situation through a clearer lens.

This is not about excusing what was done. It is not about shrinking the offense or denying your hurt. It is not about calling something harmful acceptable. Understanding is not excusing. Understanding is seeing clearly. It is stepping out of the fog of pain long enough to recognize the humanity of the person who caused it.

Sometimes people hurt others not because they are evil, but because they are wounded. They act from pain they have never faced, brokenness they have never healed, and sin they have never surrendered. It is one of the hard truths of relationships that hurt people hurt people. Broken people break others. Unhealed hearts often bleed on the innocent. Seeing that does not remove accountability, but it allows compassion to exist alongside justice. It lets the heart breathe again, and it opens space for forgiveness to become possible.

Seeing Their Humanity

When your heart is wounded, it is easy to make the offender bigger than human. Pain magnifies what they did. Betrayal makes them look heartless. Disappointment paints them as uncaring. Silence makes them seem indifferent. But most people are not as simple as the pain they cause. They carry histories that shape them. They have their own wounds, upbringing, traumas, struggles, and blind spots.

You may be hurt by someone who is hurting. You may be abandoned by someone who never learned how to stay. You may be betrayed by someone who grows up around betrayal. You may be spoken to harshly by someone who is never spoken to gently. You may be judged by someone who has never learned grace. Seeing their humanity does not justify what they did. But it helps explain where it comes from. It helps you understand that their actions rise from their weakness, not from your worth.

Some wounds are not even intentional. Some people do not mean to hurt you. They are not malicious, they are blind. They are not cruel, they are careless. They are not calculating, they are simply unhealed. When you understand that, your heart starts letting go of the need to personalize everything.

Understanding Helps You Drop the Self Blame

One of the most damaging things about hurt is how quickly it turns inward. Your mind starts asking questions it cannot answer fairly. Was I not enough. Did I deserve this. Could I have prevented it. What did I do wrong. Pain makes you believe you caused what happened, even when you did not.

Understanding the offender helps you step out of misplaced guilt. It reminds you that people's actions come from what is happening inside them, not from what is lacking in you. You are not responsible for their immaturity, their unhealed wounds, their fears, or their failures. You do not cause their insecurity or create their brokenness. Their choices belong to them.

When your heart sees that, it stops carrying shame that never belonged to it. It stops trying to rewrite the past by blaming itself. Forgiveness feels lighter when you know the wound is never a reflection of your value.

Understanding Breaks the Bitterness Cycle

Bitterness grows best in misunderstanding. When you only see someone through the lens of pain, bitterness feels justified. You replay the moment over and over, and anger rewrites the meaning each time. You start defining them by their worst action. You hold them hostage to one moment in time.

Understanding softens the ground bitterness grows in. It does not erase what is wrong, but it weakens resentment's grip. It allows compassion to enter places bitterness tries to occupy. It keeps your heart from turning cold, hardened, or cynical.

Unforgiveness often grows into bitterness, and bitterness can grow into paranoia, a constant expectation of pain. Understanding disrupts that pattern. It reminds you the world is not full of enemies. It reminds you that one person hurting you does not mean everyone will. It pulls your heart out of bitterness and back into perspective.

Understanding Loosens the Need for Revenge

Revenge can feel like a natural response to deep hurt. Something inside you wants them to feel what you felt. It wants them to understand the cost. It can feel like justice, but it is also bondage. Revenge ties your healing to their suffering, and it keeps you emotionally chained to the person you want to be free from.

Understanding does not cancel accountability, but it loosens the craving for revenge. When you see their brokenness, you remember that God sees too. God knows. God handles justice with perfect wisdom.

Even if you could hurt them back, it would not cancel what happened to you. Revenge cannot heal the wound. It only deepens it. Understanding restores clarity by reminding you that your healing is not dependent on someone else's suffering. It frees you from carrying that exhausting desire to see them pay.

Understanding Does Not Cancel Boundaries

This part matters, so I want to say it plainly. Understanding someone does not mean staying close to them. Understanding is not reconciliation. Understanding does not invite them back into your heart. It does not erase the need for wisdom, safety, distance, or boundaries.

You can understand someone and still choose not to trust them again. You can understand someone and still protect your heart. You can understand someone and still walk away. You can understand someone and accept that the relationship will never be the same.

Understanding frees your heart, not your boundaries. Forgiveness opens the door for healing. Wisdom closes the door to repeated harm.

Understanding Brings God Into the Story

When you begin to understand the other person, even a little, something spiritual shifts. The story stops being you versus them, and it becomes you and God walking through this together. Understanding shifts the focus from what they did to what God is doing in you.

You start noticing ways God protects you, even when you do not see it at the time. You start recognizing how He is restoring you in quiet places you almost overlook. You begin to see that God is using the pain to grow you, refine you, and draw you closer to Himself. Understanding does not glorify the offense. It glorifies the God who heals.

And maybe the most beautiful part of understanding is what it prepares in you. It makes forgiveness possible, not because the offender becomes innocent, but because your heart becomes free. Not because they apologize, but because your eyes open. Not because they change, but because God is changing you.

Understanding becomes a bridge between the wound and the healing. It becomes the doorway to forgiveness and the start of emotional release. It is the moment the heart stops fighting the past and begins moving toward the future. And in that place, forgiveness is still hard, but it becomes possible. It can even start feeling gentle and sacred.

Chapter 9: Choosing Forgiveness
Even Before You Feel It

F orgiveness begins long before the heart feels ready. It starts in that quiet place of obedience, right in the middle of life, when you realize healing doesn't come from waiting for emotions to change. It comes from surrendering those emotions to God. A lot of people picture forgiveness as a sudden wave of relief, like peace just rushes in and everything feels lighter. But most of the time, forgiveness doesn't start with peace. It starts with a decision, and that decision can feel unnatural, uncomfortable, and sometimes even unfair.

The heart wants to forgive after it feels healed. God invites us to forgive so healing can begin. That difference matters more than we realize. It draws the line between emotional bondage and emotional freedom. It also explains why forgiveness takes faith more than it takes feeling. If we had to wait to feel better before forgiving, we might never forgive at all, because pain often doesn't lift until forgiveness begins. Feelings respond to forgiveness. They don't lead it. Forgiveness is the seed, and peace is the fruit, and the seed has to be planted first.

There are moments in every believer's life when forgiveness feels impossible. Not because you don't want to do what's right, but because the wound feels too deep, the memory too fresh, or the betrayal too heavy. In those moments, obedience feels like climbing uphill with a weight on your back. But God never calls us to something He won't empower. When He calls you to forgive, He supplies grace, strength, and clarity to walk that road.

That's why Jesus talks about forgiveness as a spiritual discipline, not an emotional suggestion. When Peter asks how many times forgiveness is required, Jesus gives an answer that sounds impossible on purpose. He's not trying to overwhelm Peter. He's showing him that forgiveness can't depend on emotion. It has to rest on obedience.

Forgiveness Starts With a Decision

Forgiveness isn't something that just happens to you. It's something you choose. It's that quiet declaration you make to God, even if your faith is shaking. You tell Him you choose to forgive. And honestly, those words can feel strange the first time you say them. You might feel anger rise as you pray. You might feel tears pushing forward. You might feel your body resist and your mind protest.

Still, heaven responds to obedience, not emotional readiness. Forgiveness is an act of will before it becomes a spiritual experience. The miracle comes after the choice, not before it. Peace enters after obedience. Healing begins after surrender. You choose the path, and God walks it with you until your emotions catch up with the truth you've declared.

Forgiveness isn't a feeling. It's a decision to release the trauma and the offense into God's hands. That choice is part of emotional and spiritual maturity, doing what's right even when your heart is still catching its breath.

Why Feelings Push Back

Feelings resist forgiveness because they are shaped by the wound. They form in moments of pain, betrayal, loss, and disappointment. Feelings stay loyal to memory. They cling to the version of the story that once kept you safe, even when that version is now keeping you stuck. They replay the hurt to protect you from being hurt again. But what protected you yesterday can imprison you today.

That's why God doesn't ask your feelings for permission. He asks your obedience for participation. When your will aligns with God's instruction, your heart eventually follows. Sometimes it takes days. Sometimes it takes weeks or longer. But healing comes.

When you forgive, anger and resentment lose their place to live. They have nothing left to grip. Bitterness can't thrive in a heart that surrenders the offense to God. Resentment weakens when obedience takes root. Forgiveness slowly dismantles the emotional structures that keep pain alive.

The Trap of Waiting for an Apology

Many people delay forgiveness because they're waiting for the offender to own what they did. They tell themselves they will forgive after the apology comes. Or they believe their heart will soften once the other person finally acknowledges the damage. But apologies are unpredictable. Some people never apologize, not because you don't deserve one, but because they can't give what they've never learned.

Waiting for an apology gives the offender power over your healing. It ties your freedom to their repentance. It makes your peace depend on their humility. That's too much power to hand to any human being.

Not everyone comes back to ask for forgiveness. And some who hurt you may never understand the weight of what they caused. That truth hurts, but it also frees you. If forgiveness doesn't depend on them, then healing stays between you and God. That means the door to your healing is never locked. It stays open.

Forgiveness becomes possible when you stop waiting for someone else to release you and choose to release yourself.

What Shifts When You Declare Forgiveness

Something real happens the moment you tell God you forgive someone. You might not feel different right away. The memory might still sting. Your emotions might still be raw. But something shifts in the spiritual realm. Something loosens. Something lifts. Something breaks.

Even if the other person never knows what you've done, heaven knows. Even if your feelings don't lighten immediately, your spirit knows. Forgiveness begins working the moment you declare it. Your emotions eventually realize the war is over. Your mind eventually stops defending the wound. Your heart eventually stops bleeding. But the declaration comes first.

Forgiveness can start privately, even if the offender is nowhere near you. It can be spoken with your mouth in prayer, even if it never reaches their ears. That's powerful, because it means forgiveness lives between you and God before it touches anything else. Healing begins even when reconciliation is impossible.

Forgiveness Is Faith in Action

Forgiveness is one of the purest acts of faith because it asks you to trust that God will take what you surrender and transform it. You might not see how yet. You might not know when. But you choose to believe that God handles justice with wisdom, heals your heart with patience, and redeems your story with love.

At its core, forgiveness says you trust God more than you trust your pain. It says God sees more. He understands more. He reaches places in you that you can't reach on your own. Forgiveness is worship. It's obedience. It's trust. It's surrender. And it's freedom.

When Obedience Comes First

There comes a day when your emotions catch up with your obedience. The memory still exists, but the sting fades. The story stays the same, but the pain doesn't rule you anymore. You remember without reliving. You speak about it without shaking. You think about it without bleeding.

That transformation can be slow, gentle, and sacred. It's the Spirit of God working inside you over time. But it starts with a choice. A hard, sacrificial, holy choice that says you choose forgiveness because you choose God. Then, little by little, your emotions surrender. Bitterness dissolves. Resentment weakens. Anger softens. Peace returns.

This is the beauty of choosing forgiveness before you feel it. Healing starts even when your heart hasn't fully noticed yet. Your healing isn't tied to a feeling. It's tied to a choice. And your choice is tied to God.

Chapter 10: Letting Go Of The Debt

O ne of the most powerful truths about forgiveness is that it always involves releasing a debt. Every offense creates some kind of emotional debt, whether the hurt feels big or small. Something inside you starts believing the person owes you. Maybe it's an apology. Maybe it's an explanation. Maybe it's changed behavior. Sometimes it's as simple as wanting them to feel the weight of what they did. But forgiveness means you release that debt. You come to terms with the fact that even if they gave you everything you think you need, it still would not fully fix what happened. Forgiveness is letting go of the expectation that they must pay for your pain.

That's hard because the heart naturally longs for justice. When someone wounds you, something deep in you cries out for fairness. You want the wrong acknowledged. You want the pain validated. You want truth to be named, and you want the emotional balance restored. You want back what was taken from you.

The tragedy is that many people spend their whole lives waiting for repayment that never comes. Some offenders refuse to admit they did anything wrong. Others minimize it or justify it. Some never realize the damage they cause. Some are so broken that they can't give you what you need, even if they wanted to. When your healing is tied to their repentance, your heart stays trapped by their choices.

Holding on to pain and anger keeps the wrongdoer close to your heart, and it destroys you while they remain unaffected. That is what unforgiveness does. It tethers you to a moment you cannot change. It chains your emotions to someone who may already move on. It binds your heart to a person who may not even remember what they did. Releasing the debt is not about setting them free. It is about setting you free.

The Weight of Emotional Debt

Emotional debt is heavy. It sits on your heart like an invisible weight and shapes how you breathe, think, and feel. When you hold someone in emotional debt, you carry them with you everywhere. You bring them into new relationships and new conversations. You bring them into your joy and your future. Even when you don't mean to, they keep showing up inside you.

That weight gets even heavier when you constantly watch the life of the person who hurt you. You notice their smiles, their successes, their good moments, and it stings because they seem fine while you feel like you're still bleeding. Emotional debt makes you expect life to punish them, humble them, or break them the way they broke you. But life does not always unfold like that. Watching them do well while you struggle only deepens the wound.

That's why the debt has to be released. As long as you hold them accountable in your heart, you stay tied to their journey, their growth, or their lack of it. You stay emotionally entangled in a life that is no longer your responsibility.

Letting Go Means Accepting the Past Cannot Change

Letting go is really about facing a painful truth. What happened cannot be undone. You can't rewrite that moment. You can't go back and protect yourself. You can't unsay the words or unlive the betrayal. The past is fixed, but your relationship to the past doesn't have to stay the same.

Releasing the debt means separating your identity from what was done to you. It means refusing to let one moment control the rest of your life. It means choosing to stop walking back into the same memory hoping it will finally give you closure. Repetition doesn't heal anything. It just revives the pain. Letting go steps out of the loop and says, I can't change what happened, but I can change what it holds over me. That's where God meets you and heals what is still tender.

Letting Go Is Not Forgetting

A lot of people fear letting go because they think it means forgetting. They worry that if they release the debt, they dishonor their pain or pretend the offense isn't serious. But letting go is not forgetting. Forgetting isn't required, and it usually isn't realistic. The mind does not erase emotional events, and God does not ask it to.

Letting go doesn't delete the memory. It removes the power the memory has to control your life. It doesn't deny what happened. It restores your heart's relationship to what happened. You still remember, but you remember differently. Instead of tension, peace grows. Instead of anger, clarity grows. Instead of resentment, strength grows. Instead of endless tears, your story starts carrying meaning.

Justice and Trusting God With It

Every heart cries out for justice. That's natural because we are made in the image of a just God. But human justice and divine justice don't work the same way. Human justice wants immediate balance. It wants an apology, a consequence, a clear admission of wrong. Divine justice sees the whole story, including what we can't see yet.

Releasing the debt means trusting that God sees everything. He knows what is hidden. He judges with fairness. He restores what is lost in ways you may not expect. Letting go is not trusting the offender. It is trusting God. It is recognizing the wound is bigger than the moment itself, and God is working in you in ways pain cannot stop.

Letting Go Frees You More Than It Costs You

When you release someone from emotional debt, it can feel like you're losing something. You might feel like you're giving up your rightness, your claim to justice, or the last thread connecting you to what mattered. But forgiveness isn't a loss. It's a liberation.

You lose bitterness, resentment, heaviness, sleepless nights, and the mental replay that keeps dragging you back. You lose the tightness you feel when their name comes up or their face crosses your mind. In that space, you gain peace, clarity, joy, freedom, healing, and God's nearness. You gain yourself back. Releasing the debt is not about what you lose. It's about what you recover.

Letting Go Does Not Require Reconciliation

Another fear people carry is that letting go means reopening the relationship. But forgiveness doesn't require reconciliation. Some relationships can be restored, and some can't. Some should, and some shouldn't. Forgiveness isn't deciding the future of the relationship. It's deciding the condition of your heart.

You can release the debt and still keep boundaries. You can forgive and still choose distance. You can let go and still walk away. Letting go isn't about restoring the relationship. It's about restoring you.

Letting Go Starts With a Simple Confession

Letting go often begins with a simple, sacred confession to God that you forgive. Those words don't excuse what happened. They don't justify it. They don't minimize it. They simply release it. They tell heaven and your own soul that you refuse to stay tied to the wound.

Releasing the debt is one of the deepest forms of forgiveness because it admits the truth. Nothing the offender gives can fully balance what is lost. Only God restores what is taken. Only God heals what is wounded. Only God redeems what is broken. And the moment you release that debt, God begins the work that only He can do.

Chapter 11: The Difference Between Forgiving And Rebuilding

F orgiveness and trust get mentioned in the same breath all the time, but they are not the same thing. Forgiveness is something God calls you to do. Trust is something that gets rebuilt over time. You can forgive in a moment, but trust takes a process. Forgiveness is unconditional. Trust is not. You can forgive someone fully and still decide they are not safe to trust again. You can release the pain and still not restore the relationship. You can open your heart to healing without reopening the door to the person who hurt you.

This is where a lot of people get stuck. They fear that forgiving someone means going back to the same closeness, the same openness, the same vulnerability. But God never commands you to trust everyone. He commands you to love and to forgive. Trust is something He wants you to give wisely. It is earned, not automatic. It is a gift, and it has to be stewarded well. When someone has proved they won't protect your heart, wisdom says you don't keep handing them access.

Forgiving does not mean forgetting. Forgiving does not mean allowing someone to keep hurting you. Some hurts can't be undone, and some relationships can't be rebuilt in a healthy way. Forgiveness is for your freedom. Trust is rebuilt only if the person, and the

89

relationship, are safe enough for that kind of restoration.

Forgiveness Deals With the Heart, Trust Deals With Behavior

Forgiveness is about the past. Trust is about the future. Forgiveness releases the emotional debt of what happened. Trust looks at what happens next and asks, can I walk with this person again without getting wounded the same way.

When trust is broken, it can't be patched with words alone. It doesn't come back just because someone says they're sorry. Real trust needs consistency, humility, accountability, genuine change, and time. Words may explain regret, but actions reveal repentance. Someone can say the right thing once, but trust grows when their life keeps showing the right thing over and over.

Forgiveness says, you don't owe me anything anymore. Trust says, show me you are safe enough to walk with again. Those can exist together without conflict.

Reconciliation Isn't Always Required

Here's something believers often need to hear clearly. Reconciliation is not always possible, and it isn't always healthy. Forgiveness can happen whether reconciliation happens or not. Forgiveness frees you. Reconciliation requires both people willing to rebuild something new.

Some offenders never acknowledge what they did. Others acknowledge it but don't change. Some relationships are too toxic to rebuild. Some spaces are too unsafe to return to. Some people are not stable enough to be allowed back into your heart. In those cases, God doesn't require you to walk back into harm just because you forgave.

You can forgive deeply and still choose distance. You can release the pain and still protect your wellbeing. Forgiveness is personal liberation. It's a choice you make before God for the sake of your soul, not a promise to restore a relationship at any cost. Reconciliation needs wisdom, not just willingness.

Trust Comes Back Slowly

Trust is not a door you fling open all at once. It returns gradually. It comes back when someone shows change, not when they promise change. It comes back when they understand what they did, not when they defend themselves. It comes back when they respect your healing instead of demanding quick closeness.

If someone tells you that you should trust them because you forgave them, they don't understand trust. They want the benefits of closeness without carrying the responsibility of rebuilding it. Trust requires humility. A broken relationship doesn't heal through pressure, pretending, or rushing. Trust grows when the person who broke it becomes someone who can hold it again.

Apologies help, but they are not enough by themselves. Trust grows through patience, accountability, and consistent fruit. There is no shortcut here. The process has to be walked with honesty and boundaries that protect your healing.

Trust Needs Evidence of Change

You are not responsible for the offender's healing. But if reconciliation is possible, there will be signs that their healing is real. Change shows up through consistency. A person who is truly growing doesn't demand trust. They earn it. They don't minimize the pain. They acknowledge it. They don't blame circumstances. They take responsibility. They don't repeat the wound. They honor your boundaries. They stay patient with your process.

Real repentance isn't proven by emotion alone. Anyone can cry. Anyone can feel guilt. Repentance shows itself in transformation, in the way they live, speak, choose, and react. If those signs are missing, reconciliation becomes unwise, even if forgiveness is already present.

Forgiveness Without Trust Still Heals You

Some people think forgiveness is incomplete unless the relationship gets rebuilt. That's not true. Forgiveness is complete when you release the debt and hand the pain to God. Rebuilding the relationship is a separate journey, and sometimes it doesn't happen. You can forgive entirely and still decide the relationship can't continue.

You can close a chapter with dignity. You can love from a distance. You can pray for someone without giving them access. You can bless them without inviting them back. Forgiveness is unconditional. Trust is selective. Forgiveness is required. Reconciliation is optional. Trust is earned. Knowing this protects you from unnecessary pressure. It frees you from trying to repair something God may be asking you to release.

God Heals Even When the Relationship Can't Be Restored

Some wounds don't get fixed through reconciliation. Sometimes the relationship ends permanently. Sometimes the person passes away. Sometimes the damage is too deep. Sometimes distance is God's protection. But healing is still possible because healing is tied to God's presence, not the offender's presence.

God heals hearts that choose freedom even when they don't get closure. He restores joy even when the relationship cannot be restored. He redeems pain even when the story doesn't end the way you wish it did. He isn't limited by human refusal or hindered by someone else's stubbornness. He can complete what they leave unfinished.

When Trust Can Be Rebuilt

There are times when reconciliation is possible. Sometimes the offender is repentant, humbled, transformed, and willing to rebuild. In those moments, trust can return, but it still returns carefully, prayerfully, and in stages.

Trust rebuilds when both hearts commit to honesty. It grows when accountability becomes normal. It strengthens when the offender understands what was broken and respects the pace required to repair it. It flourishes when both people listen deeply and walk humbly.

Even then, trust rises slowly. It cannot be rushed or demanded. If God is leading reconciliation, He also guides the pace. He gives peace about when to step forward and when to pause. Trust rebuilt with God becomes stronger than trust rebuilt without Him.

Your Responsibility Is Forgiveness, Not the Outcome

One of the freedoms God gives in forgiveness is clarity about what belongs to you and what doesn't. You are responsible for forgiving. You are responsible for healing and surrendering your pain to God. But you are not responsible for the offender's response. You are not responsible for their remorse. You are not responsible for their growth. And you aren't responsible for reconciliation unless God clearly leads you into it.

You can control your heart. You cannot control theirs. You can release your pain. You cannot force their change. You can heal your wound. You cannot heal their broken places. Forgiveness sets you free from carrying what was never yours to carry. Trust is a gift you give only to those God shows are safe enough to hold it.

Chapter 12: Setting Boundaries That Heal, Not Harm

B oundaries are not walls built out of bitterness. They are fences built out of wisdom. They don't say, I reject you. They say, I respect myself. They don't say, I'm punishing you. They say, I'm protecting what God is healing in me. When you set boundaries, you honor God by stewarding your emotional and spiritual health, and you honor yourself by refusing to sit again in places where you once bled.

Healing Makes Boundaries Necessary

After a wound heals, it can feel tender for a while. A heart that forgives becomes soft again, not weak, but renewed. It starts to feel again. It starts to breathe again. But tenderness needs protection, or it gets bruised by old patterns and familiar pain.

That's why boundaries matter. Without them, forgiveness stays fragile. Without them, old wounds reopen. Without them, the offender can repeat the same patterns, sometimes without even realizing it. And without them, you can find yourself pulled back into cycles God already brings you out of. Some wounds grow deeper simply because people confuse forgiveness with access, love with vulnerability, and grace with exposure. But healing changes you, and that change comes with responsibility. Once your heart is mended, it needs tending.

Boundaries Teach People How to Treat You

People often treat you according to the standards you set. When someone has repeated access to your heart with no boundaries, they learn that you tolerate what hurts you. Most of the time they don't keep wounding you because they are plotting against you. They keep doing it because they are allowed to.

But when you set boundaries, you teach others that your heart is valuable. You teach them your presence is a privilege, not a guarantee. You teach them respect is required, not optional. Boundaries redefine the terms of the relationship. They create clarity, and clarity is what makes any healthy reconciliation possible.

You can't keep letting someone wound you and call it forgiveness. Setting boundaries isn't unforgiveness. It's maturity. It's saying, I forgive you, and I'm still going to walk in wisdom. Forgiveness releases the debt. Boundaries keep new debts from forming.

Boundaries Look Different for Different Relationships

Not every relationship needs the same boundaries. Some relationships can be restored with soft boundaries. Others need firm ones. Some require distance. Others require accountability. Some need a pause. Others need a permanent separation. Boundaries aren't one-size-fits-all. They are shaped carefully, prayerfully, and honestly.

With a spouse, boundaries might look like structured

communication or stronger emotional honesty. With a parent, they might mean limiting certain topics or adjusting how often you connect. With a friend, boundaries might mean redefining expectations or creating healthier space. With a former partner or a toxic person, boundaries might mean full distance. Every boundary is shaped by the depth of the wound, the other person's willingness to change, and the direction God gives you. Your heart belongs to God, not to the one who hurt you, and your boundaries decide who gets to approach that sacred place.

Boundaries Protect the Fruit of Forgiveness

When God heals your heart, peace starts coming back. You feel lighter. Clearer. Stronger. But peace can be delicate, and it needs protection from environments, conversations, and relationships that disturb it.

Boundaries keep you from returning to places where peace can't grow. They guard your joy from people who drain it. They shield your mind from voices that pull you into doubt. They protect your spirit from constant offense. Forgiveness gives you peace, and boundaries help you keep it. Boundaries also help you move forward with wisdom instead of fear. They let you love from a healed place, not a wounded one.

Boundaries Are Not Meant to Punish

Boundaries are not revenge. They are not meant to shout, you hurt me so now you suffer. Boundaries are neutral until intention is added. When they come from anger, they turn into walls. When they come from fear, they turn into avoidance. But when they come from wisdom and love, they become tools of healing.

They don't punish the offender. They protect the one who is healing. And sometimes they protect the offender too, because they stop harmful behavior from continuing. Boundaries teach responsibility. They create space for reflection. They give room for change. They invite maturity. Boundaries held in love can strengthen a relationship. Boundaries held in bitterness can harden a heart. The difference is the posture. Forgiveness prepares the heart. Boundaries preserve it.

God Uses Boundaries to Guide Your Steps

There's a spiritual side to boundaries that people sometimes overlook. When God restores a heart, He also guides that heart into new habits, new environments, and sometimes new relationships. Boundaries, when they're set with prayer and discernment, help you stay aligned with God's direction.

God may lead you away from certain people for a season. He may move you closer to others. He may tell you to limit certain conversations, protect your time, or step back from voices that keep stirring old wounds. These are boundaries shaped by the Holy Spirit. What God heals, He also guards. What God restores, He also protects. Your boundaries are part of how He keeps you safe.

Boundaries Help You Become Who God Calls You to Be

Healing isn't the finish line. Healing is the start of becoming.

As you forgive and set boundaries, you step into the person God calls you to be, someone confident, peaceful, discerning, loving, and whole.

Boundaries help you grow because they create space. They give you room to reflect, breathe, and listen to what's happening in your heart without pressure. Forgiveness shapes you into a wiser, stronger version of yourself. Boundaries protect that growth. They keep old patterns from interrupting what God is building in you. And as you grow, your boundaries grow too. What you need in one season might change in the next, because healing keeps moving you forward.

Boundaries Are Acts of Love

At their core, boundaries are about love. Love for God, love for yourself, and sometimes even love for the other person. When boundaries come from a clean heart, they honor what God is doing in you. They say, I value what God restores too much to let it be damaged again.

Boundaries say your heart matters. Your peace matters. Your healing matters. What God restores will not be casually broken again. Forgiveness sets your heart free. Boundaries help it stay free. Together they make healing something sustainable, not something temporary.

Chapter 13: Healing Conversations

There comes a point in the forgiveness journey when a conversation needs to happen. Not to reopen the wound, but to release the weight it has carried for so long. Healing conversations aren't like everyday conversations. They come from a softer heart, a quieter mind, and a spirit steadied by God. They don't come from emotional overflow. They come from emotional clarity. The goal isn't to accuse. The goal is to heal.

When we talk while we're still bleeding, communication gets messy. Words coming from a wounded place are rarely clean. They come out sharp, defensive, reactive, and unfiltered. We often speak before we really understand what we feel, and in that confusion, more damage happens. Hurt can make the heart suspicious. You start imagining motives, assuming intentions, and interpreting silence as rejection. When the heart is wounded, communication bends out of shape. You're not really speaking from truth. You're speaking from the tremble of the injury.

That's why healing has to begin before the conversation does. You can't build reconciliation on broken words. You can't repair a relationship with an unhealed heart. Healing conversations need preparation, spiritually, emotionally, and sometimes even physically. You come to the table not demanding restoration, but willing to extend compassion. The conversation may not change the other person, but it changes you. It may not fix the relationship, but it frees your soul.

Healing Conversations Start With God

Before you speak to the person who hurt you, you talk to God first. He's the One who steadies your emotions, shows you your blind spots, softens your tone, and gives you the wisdom to say what's really in your heart. Prayer purifies motives. It pulls out the desire for revenge and replaces it with the desire for peace. It quiets the storm so your words don't come out like thunder.

Sometimes you don't even know what you feel until you bring it to God. That's why prayer matters so much. Sometimes the Holy Spirit makes it clear that a conversation isn't necessary. Sometimes He shows you the timing is off. Sometimes He tells you to wait. And sometimes He surprises you by opening a door for reconciliation you didn't think was possible. Healing conversations don't begin with your mouth. They begin with your heart laid open before God.

Timing Matters More Than We Think

Not every moment is the right moment for a healing conversation. Some conversations happen too early, when emotions are high and clarity is low. Others happen too late, after distance has already reshaped the relationship. Timing takes discernment.

There's wisdom in waiting for the heart to settle. There's also wisdom in not delaying forever. Conversations that come too soon can do harm, but conversations that never come can leave long, silent fractures. Discernment helps you know the difference.

Pain can make us rush into conversations we aren't ready for, hoping the talk itself will heal us. But no conversation heals what hasn't been surrendered to God. Healing leads communication. Communication doesn't lead healing. So wait until you can speak without shaking. Wait until your voice carries truth more than tears. Wait until you can name your pain without getting lost in it. Wait until you can listen without planning a rebuttal. Most importantly, wait until your goal is peace, not victory.

Clarity Is More Important Than Emotion

Healing conversations need clarity. When you speak from a healed or healing place, your words come out gentle but firm, honest but kind, vulnerable but grounded. You stop attacking the person. You simply express the truth of your experience.

Unspoken hurt tends to rot into bitterness or self-punishment. A healing conversation gives truth a place to breathe so bitterness doesn't grow in silence. It gives you a way to say how their actions affected you, not to accuse them, but to release what you've been carrying. It also gives them a chance to see what they might miss.

Clarity isn't cold. Clarity is compassionate. Clear words help the listener stay less defensive. They don't feel attacked, they feel informed. They don't feel blamed, they feel invited into understanding. A healing conversation isn't about proving you're right. It's about sharing your truth in a way that honors your healing and respects the other person's journey.

Listening Is Part of the Work

A healing conversation is never one-sided. Even if you're the one who was hurt, listening becomes part of your healing. You're not listening to excuse what happened. You're listening to understand, because understanding often brings closure.

Sometimes you discover they had no idea the pain went that deep. Other times you find out they were fighting battles you never saw. That context doesn't erase the wound, but it can explain things, and explanation brings clarity. You begin to see that sometimes people hurt us unintentionally, out of ignorance, immaturity, or unhealed places. Understanding that helps you detach the pain from your identity. You realize they didn't hurt you because you are unworthy. They hurt you because they are unhealed.

Listening doesn't weaken your position. It strengthens your understanding. It lets your heart soften without turning naïve. It brings balance to the story pain keeps trying to tell.

You Accept Even If You Don't Agree

One of the hardest parts of healing conversations is accepting that the response may not be what you hope for. They may not understand fully. They may not take responsibility. They may minimize your experience. They may deflect or shift blame. That hurts, but it doesn't cancel your healing.

A healing conversation isn't about controlling the outcome.

It's about expressing your truth with grace and then handing the outcome back to God. You can't choose their reaction, but you can choose your release. You can choose peace even if they stay defensive. You can choose closure even if they offer none. You can choose healing even if there's no apology.

Forgiveness doesn't depend on their apology. And the value of the conversation isn't found in their words. It's found in your posture. The conversation may not change them, but it changes you.

Sometimes Conversations Rebuild, Sometimes They Close

There are times when a healing conversation becomes the first step toward reconciliation. When both hearts are open, humility is present, and understanding flows, a relationship can be restored in a deeper, more honest way. A conversation like that can melt years of distance, clear old misunderstanding, and bring light where silence used to rule. When God sits at the center of the table, those conversations feel sacred. Love rises over pain. Truth rises over pride. Forgiveness rises over distance.

But there are also times when healing conversations don't restore the relationship. Instead, they bring closure. And closure is still healing. It's emotional freedom returning. It's the quiet acceptance that the relationship can't move forward, but your heart can. Closure isn't failure. Closure is a gift. Some relationships need to end for the heart to breathe again. Forgiveness is for the soul, not for forcing a relationship to survive. Healing conversations help you walk away with peace instead of bitterness, and clarity instead of confusion.

Healing Conversations Come After Healing Hearts

You can't speak healing from a wounded place. You speak healing from a surrendered place. That's why healing conversations follow forgiveness, not the other way around. Forgiveness prepares the heart. Boundaries protect it. Healing conversations express what God is already transforming inside you.

When you speak from healing, your voice carries grace. Your words carry truth. Your heart carries peace. And whether the conversation restores the relationship or releases it, you walk away whole.

Chapter 14: Reconciliation: When It Is Possible & When It Isn't

R econciliation often gets treated like the final step of forgiveness. It's pictured as the moment hearts reunite, misunderstandings fade, and everything settles back into harmony. A lot of people even measure forgiveness by whether reconciliation happens. If the relationship isn't restored, they assume forgiveness must be incomplete. But that idea causes so much unnecessary pressure, and it can be one of the most expensive misunderstandings in healing.

Forgiveness and reconciliation are connected, but they're not the same thing. Forgiveness is your responsibility. Reconciliation is a shared possibility. Forgiveness is something God commands. Reconciliation is conditional. Forgiveness can be one-sided. Reconciliation needs two willing hearts. Forgiveness frees your spirit. Reconciliation restores a relationship only if it's healthy enough to hold what comes next.

Forgiveness is personal liberation, and reconciliation should never be forced. Holding on to pain chains us to the people who hurt us, but reconciling without wisdom can wound us all over again. That tension matters because the truth is simple and painful at the same time. Some relationships can be reconciled, and others can't, and both outcomes can still lead to real healing.

Reconciliation Needs Two Changed Hearts

Reconciliation isn't about going back to the way things used to be. It's about building something new. A relationship that heals after harm is a relationship rebuilt on honesty, humility, and renewed trust. That only happens when both people are willing to face what happened, take responsibility, and pursue a healthier future.

Reconciliation can't grow if the offender refuses accountability. It can't grow if the behaviors stay the same. It can't grow if the environment is unsafe. It can't grow if the relationship still asks you to betray yourself just to keep the peace. One of the biggest dangers in healing is mistaking forgiveness for invitation. Forgiving someone doesn't automatically give them access to your life again. Access comes after responsibility, maturity, and consistent change. Without those things, reconciliation becomes exposure, not restoration.

Letting go doesn't always mean returning. Some relationships do more damage when we step back into them too quickly. That's why reconciliation isn't proof that forgiveness is real. Wisdom is.

The Pain of Forcing Reconciliation

There's a specific kind of pain that shows up when you try to force a relationship back together. It happens when you want reconciliation more than the other person does. It happens when you keep hoping for change that never comes. It happens when you silence your own needs just to keep things calm. It happens when you accept unhealthy patterns because you're afraid of what distance might mean.

Forced reconciliation isn't healing. It's emotional self-abandonment. You can forgive someone and still feel disappointed that reconciliation doesn't unfold the way you want. You can feel like you failed, or like you weren't spiritual enough, or like you're supposed to keep reopening your heart to harm. But forgiveness isn't the same as self-neglect. Returning to an environment God pulls you out of isn't faith. It's danger. Reconciliation should never cost you your peace, your safety, or your identity.

When Reconciliation Is Safe, It's Beautiful

When reconciliation is truly possible, it becomes one of the clearest pictures of grace. Two people name the wound. Two hearts humble themselves. Two souls soften. Something new forms, and it's often stronger than what existed before because it's refined by truth.

Reconciliation built on repentance becomes a testimony. Reconciliation built on honesty brings strength. Reconciliation built on love creates healing. Sometimes relationships even grow deeper after forgiveness because both people learn compassion and understanding in a way they didn't have before. But even then, reconciliation needs time. It grows gently. It's nurtured, not rushed. It's tested, not assumed. Healing leads the pace, and God leads the direction.

Healing Does Not Depend on Reconciliation

There's a sacred kind of peace that comes when you realize you can heal without reconciling. You can forgive without returning. You can release pain without keeping connection. You can close a chapter without revisiting it.

This matters especially when you've faced deep betrayal, manipulation, or ongoing abuse. Some relationships can't be restored, not because God is powerless, but because human will is involved. God doesn't force people to change. He invites them, convicts them, and works in them, but He doesn't override their freedom. If someone refuses accountability, refuses honesty, or refuses to acknowledge the wound, reconciliation becomes unwise. Healing needs distance. Peace needs separation. Growth needs release.

Reconciliation isn't always possible, and when you accept that, you stop blaming yourself. A lot of people carry guilt over relationships that end. They assume a lack of reconciliation means their forgiveness is shallow. But forgiveness shouldn't be measured by whether the relationship survives. It should be measured by whether peace returns to your heart.

Signs Reconciliation Is Unsafe

Sometimes the wisest thing you can do is step back. Reconciliation is unsafe when the person still minimizes your pain. It's unsafe when they deny responsibility. It's unsafe when they keep repeating the same patterns. It's unsafe when they demand forgiveness while refusing to change.

Some relationships only survive when the pain they cause is ignored. But reconciliation can't thrive inside denial. It needs truth. It needs courage. It needs both people facing what is real. There are moments when distance becomes the most holy decision you can make.

Letting Go Without Bitterness

One of the most freeing forms of healing is letting go without hatred. It's choosing to release resentment even when closeness can't be rebuilt. It's choosing peace over proximity. It's choosing love over bitterness. It's choosing to pray for someone even when the relationship ends.

That isn't weakness. That's maturity. That's spiritual strength. Forgiveness frees you even if the relationship can't continue. You can love from a distance, and sometimes peace comes only when you step back. Letting go without bitterness isn't cold. It's holy. It honors what God is doing in you while acknowledging the reality of the other person's choices.

God's Place in Reconciliation

Reconciliation isn't something you have to force. It's something God leads. He opens doors when it's safe. He confirms paths through peace. He softens both hearts when the time is right. And He protects you when reconciliation would only reopen what He's healing.

God doesn't lead you backward. He leads you forward. If

reconciliation belongs in your future, God orchestrates it. If it doesn't, He closes the door gently. Some wounds can't be healed by people. They can only be healed by God. And sometimes the healing He gives isn't about restoring the relationship. It's about restoring your heart.

Healing Happens Either Way

Whether reconciliation happens or not, healing is still possible. Whether the relationship survives or not, freedom is still within reach. Whether the offender returns or not, God stays faithful. Reconciliation is a blessing when it's safe, but healing is the promise. You can forgive with reconciliation. You can forgive without it. You can heal through restoration. You can heal through release. Forgiveness is certain. Reconciliation is optional. Healing is guaranteed when God is involved. No matter how your story unfolds, God leads you to peace.

Chapter 15: Rediscovering Yourself After Pain

P ain doesn't just break hearts. It messes with identity. When someone wounds you deeply, it shifts the way you see yourself. It changes how you measure your worth, your value, and even your purpose. Things you once knew with confidence suddenly feel shaky. You start wondering if you're still lovable, still enough, still worthy of kindness. Pain casts shadows in places where light used to live.

When you hold on to pain, it quietly changes you into someone you barely recognize. You grow quieter or colder. You become more cautious. You function on the outside, but you pull back on the inside. At some point you realize you don't fully recognize the person in the mirror, and that can be one of the saddest parts of the whole journey.

Forgiveness does more than release the offender. It restores you. It gives you back your voice, your light, your joy, and your sense of self. It helps you find who you are outside the wound. Pain may shake you, but healing brings you home to yourself.

Pain Changes How You See Yourself

Pain has a sneaky way of whispering lies into your identity. When you're betrayed, you start feeling unworthy. When you're abandoned, you start feeling unlovable. When you're mistreated, you feel small. When you're rejected, you feel invisible. Before long, you're measuring yourself by someone else's actions.

One of the most painful effects of hurt is how quickly we internalize it. You start believing you caused what happened. You replay conversations and moments trying to figure out what you could have done differently. But someone else's brokenness does not reflect your worth.

This identity shift feels like slow erosion. Confidence drains quietly. Joy fades bit by bit. The version of you that once felt free starts disappearing in small, almost invisible ways. Pain becomes a sculptor, chipping away at your self-esteem until you're living like a shadow of who you used to be. Healing asks you to confront that distortion. You separate what happened to you from who you are. Pain is something you experience. It is not your identity.

Forgiveness Helps You Reclaim Your Identity

When you forgive, something powerful starts happening inside you. You begin to untangle your identity from the wound. You stop seeing yourself only as someone who was hurt, and you start seeing yourself as someone who is healing. You stop looking at yourself through the offense, and you start looking at yourself through God's eyes.

Unforgiveness does more damage to you than to the offender, and one of those damages is identity loss. It ties you to the moment you were wounded. It freezes part of your sense of self in that pain. Forgiveness breaks that tie. It lifts you out of the past and sets you on a different path.

You start rediscovering your strength, your courage, your voice, and your worth. Forgiveness becomes a gift to your identity, not just your emotions.

Healing Shows You Who You Are Without the Pain

For a lot of people, pain starts shaping personality. Betrayal makes you guarded. Disappointment makes you skeptical. Disrespect makes you defensive. Rejection makes you quiet. Neglect makes you distant. Over time, these reactions feel like who you are.

But they aren't your true self. They're your wounded self. God's healing restores the real you, the you that existed before pain had a chance to reshape you. The tender you. The joyful you. The trusting you. The brave you. The loving you. The creative you. The hopeful you.

As forgiveness takes root, the parts of you that pain buried start coming back to the surface. You begin to remember that you are not defined by what happened. You are not the sum of your wounds. You are not the scar someone left behind. You are not the story another person tried to write into your soul. You are who God says you are, healed, whole, valued, and deeply loved.

Letting Go of the Version of You That Survived

Sometimes the hardest part of healing is letting go of the identity you built just to survive. Pain teaches you to armor up. It teaches you to stay alert and guarded. Those survival habits once kept you safe, but now they keep you from living fully.

Healing asks you to do something courageous. It asks you to release the version of yourself that pain shaped. That version is tired. That version is defensive. That version is always braced for impact. It's shaped by fear more than faith. It helped you get through the storm, but it can't help you flourish in peace. So you give yourself permission to outgrow it.

Rediscovering Joy

Pain steals joy quietly. It drains laughter out of places that used to feel light. It makes you suspicious of good moments. It convinces you that joy is risky, that happiness doesn't last, and that hope leads to disappointment.

But when forgiveness begins working through your heart, joy returns gently. Not with fireworks, but with small, steady steps. You smile more easily. You breathe more freely. You laugh without that shadow behind it. The heaviness lifts. Your chest feels lighter. Your heart feels safer. Joy is one of the clearest signs that healing is real. It's proof that your identity is being restored.

Rediscovering Purpose

Pain can cloud purpose. When you're wounded, most of your energy goes into surviving instead of living on purpose. You stop dreaming. You stop picturing a future you're excited about. It feels like everything narrows down to the hurt.

Healing widens your vision again. You start sensing that God still has plans for you. Possibilities you stopped believing in begin to stir again. Forgiveness creates space for new dreams because pain clutters the soul, and forgiveness clears it out. When you forgive, you make room for calling, for destiny, for the future God is still writing. Rediscovering yourself means rediscovering why you're created, and pain no longer gets to narrate that story.

Rediscovering Love

Deep hurt makes love feel complicated. You fear vulnerability. You doubt people's intentions. You prepare for danger even in safe places. Love starts feeling like a threat.

But healing softens the heart. Forgiveness loosens fear. You learn to love without losing yourself. You learn to trust wisely instead of blindly. You remember that your heart is resilient. You can love again, not because people are perfect, but because God restores what you thought you lost.

Forgiveness also brings back the ability to love yourself. Pain can convince you you're unworthy of affection, but healing reminds you that you're made for love, created in love, and sustained by love. When you rediscover love, you rediscover life.

Walking Forward as the Healed You

Rediscovering yourself after pain isn't just going back to who you were. It's becoming someone wiser, stronger, softer, and more

117

grounded. Your roots go deeper. Your compassion grows. You speak with understanding. You love without fear. You recognize your worth without needing anyone else to confirm it. You walk with confidence that comes from God, not people.

Pain tries to bury you, but healing brings you back up. Forgiveness gives you your life back. Your story isn't defined by the wound. It's defined by the restoration. Not by the fall, but by the rising. Not by the betrayal, but by the healing. And as you keep walking this road, you start seeing that forgiveness isn't only about letting go of the person who hurt you. It's also about finding yourself again.

Chapter 16: The Beauty of a Healed Heart

There is nothing as beautiful, as powerful, or as spiritually radiant as a healed heart. I'm talking about a heart that walks through pain and survives. A heart that tastes bitterness but refuses to live there. A heart that gets disappointed, betrayed, wounded, and bruised, yet still chooses love. A heart that feels shattered, but is lifted by God's hands and pieced together with grace.

The beauty of a healed heart isn't about perfection. It's about resilience. It's the softness that returns after a season of hardness. It's the openness that comes back after a season of hiding. It's the wisdom that grows after confusion. And it's the peace that settles in after turmoil.

Forgiveness doesn't only free the offender. It frees you from becoming someone you were never meant to be. That's part of the miracle of healing. It restores identity, dignity, joy, and the gentle parts of your soul that pain tries to put out.

Healed Hearts See Differently

Pain distorts vision. It makes every interaction feel risky. It makes words sound heavier than they are. It turns neutral moments into triggers. A wounded heart looks through fear, suspicion, and self-protection. You start reading meaning into things that were never meant that way. You expect hurt before it happens. You guard yourself so tightly that joy can't get in.

But healing clears your sight. When your heart heals, you start seeing people as people again, not as threats waiting to happen. You start looking at relationships with hope instead of dread. You interpret moments through reality, not memory. The fog lifts. The shadows shrink. Life starts looking brighter.

Healing lifts that emotional heaviness and makes the heart feel light again. Healed hearts don't pretend everything is perfect. They just see life accurately again.

Healed Hearts Love Freely

Pain makes love feel dangerous. After hurt, letting people in feels risky. You expect rejection. You keep parts of yourself locked away. You give carefully instead of joyfully. Love feels like a gamble, and trust feels like a mountain.

But forgiveness restores the ability to love. It brings tenderness back. It shows you that loving again isn't foolish, it's faith. It's courage. It's obedience. The healed heart opens up, not because it's naïve, but because it's redeemed. It learns that love is a gift, not a threat. When God heals your heart, He doesn't make you fragile. He makes you free.

Healed Hearts Carry Peace

Before healing, the heart lives on edge. You carry anxiety without knowing why. You replay conversations. You anticipate conflict. You question motives. Sleep gets lighter, and rest feels harder. You wonder if you'll ever feel normal again.

Peace is one of the clearest fruits of a healed heart. It isn't a life without trouble. It's calm inside you. It's quiet in the soul. It's softness in the mind. Peace becomes the atmosphere around you, replacing the chaos that once lived within.

As you let go, unseen burdens start lifting. Emotional heaviness fades. Peace settles in where confusion used to live. You breathe differently, think differently, and speak differently. This peace lasts because it's anchored in God. Scripture reminds us that God keeps those in perfect peace whose minds stay on Him, and healing draws your mind back to that place.

Healed Hearts Are Not Easily Shaken

A wounded heart reacts fast. Small shifts feel huge. One word can bruise you. A memory can knock the wind out of you. A misunderstanding can send you spiraling. But a healed heart has stability. It has roots. It has spiritual grounding.

Healing gives you emotional strength, not hardness, but strength. You don't break under small things the way you used to. You respond with wisdom rather than fear. You speak from calm rather than from reaction. Unforgiveness makes us emotional slaves, controlled by triggers and unable to rest. Healing does the opposite. It gives you authority over your reactions and places you back on steady ground. A healed heart is anchored, not in people, but in God.

Healed Hearts Become Compassionate

One of the most beautiful things about a healed heart is the compassion that comes with it. Pain can make you withdrawn and guarded. But healing expands you. It helps you recognize the pain in others. It lets you look with empathy instead of judgment.

That compassion isn't weakness. It's wisdom. You know what brokenness feels like. You've walked through valleys. You've cried tears no one sees. So you carry a soft strength people can feel.

Healing teaches you not to expect perfection from people. A healed heart gives grace because it understands human weakness. It gives space because it understands struggle. Healing doesn't make you harsher. It makes you merciful.

Healed Hearts Glow With Freedom

There's a kind of glow around a healed heart. People may not know how to name it, but they feel it. It's the glow of peace, joy, confidence, and divine restoration. A healed heart doesn't have to announce its healing. It shows up in how you live.

Forgiveness sets the soul free. The heart feels lighter. The mind feels clearer. The emotions become healthier. The spirit becomes stronger. Healing makes you feel like yourself again, not the version pain creates, not the version fear keeps alive, but the version God intends from the beginning.

Healed Hearts Become Testimonies

What God heals in you doesn't stay only with you. It becomes a testimony. It becomes hope for people still walking through their own valleys. Your healed heart tells a story without needing to speak a word.

The way you love, forgive, carry yourself, and interact with others becomes a silent sermon. It points back to God's grace. Forgiveness opens the doorway to who God designs you to be, and a healed heart is what that design looks like in real life. It shows that God doesn't only save. He restores.

The Beauty of a Heart God Touches

A healed heart is one of the most beautiful versions of you. It carries God's fingerprints. It's the fruit of His faithfulness. It's proof that your story doesn't end in pain.

You endure the wound. You walk through the valley. You surrender what hurts. You choose forgiveness. You keep saying yes to healing. And God meets you at every step.

Now you carry the beauty of restoration. It's shaped by tears, faith, surrender, and by the One who heals all wounds. A healed heart is beautiful because it knows what brokenness feels like and still chooses love. It's beautiful because it survives what should have destroyed it. It's beautiful because it reflects the God who restores it. And that beauty keeps leading you forward into the life God intends for you all along.

Chapter 17: Becoming a Vessel of Grace

T here is a transformation that happens in the life of someone who truly forgives. It is a quiet shift, a softening of spirit, a deepening of compassion. When you have walked through the valley of pain and come out healed, you carry something that knowledge alone could never give you. You carry grace. Not the shallow kind people talk about casually, but the deep and sacred kind that grows out of wounds that once felt like they would break you.

Grace is not learned in comfort. Grace is learned in sorrow. It is learned in the nights you cried alone, in the mornings you struggled to rise, in the seasons when you felt unseen and misunderstood. Grace grows in the soil of suffering. When God heals you, He does not erase the memory, He redeems it. He turns the hurt into wisdom, the tears into compassion, and the journey into a testimony.

Forgiveness brings the heart to a place where the person you used to be before the pain begins to rise again, but God does even more. He forms an upgraded version of you. You become softer and stronger, kinder and wiser, loving and discerning. And because of what you survived, you become someone God can use to bring healing to others.

Grace Comes From What You Survived

People who have never walked through deep hurt often struggle to understand those who have. But those who know suffering recognize it instantly. You can see pain in someone's eyes even behind a smile. You can hear heaviness in their voice even when their words sound steady. You notice their silence. You sense their fear. You understand them without needing a long explanation. That is grace.

Pain makes you sensitive to what others try to hide. When you have been broken, you learn to read hearts instead of just expressions. But healing turns this awareness into compassion rather than suspicion. Grace is not ignoring someone's flaws. It is understanding them. Grace does not excuse what is wrong. It simply remembers that humans fail, humans wound, humans struggle, and humans bleed. Grace sees people's failures without defining them by those failures.

This is why healed people often make the best encouragers. They know what it feels like to be overwhelmed. They know how heavy life can feel. They know the power of one kind word at the right moment. They understand how to correct with gentleness rather than condemnation. Their presence becomes safe, their words become steady, and their love becomes patient. Grace is the beauty that flows from a heart God has healed.

Grace Changes the Way You Relate to People

A healed heart interacts with others in a different way. You speak with more patience. You listen with more tenderness. You judge less quickly. You understand more deeply. You stop demanding perfection from people. You stop taking everything personally. You stop assuming the worst.

Pain once taught you to protect yourself at all costs, but healing teaches you to protect others as well. You protect their dignity. You protect their humanity. You protect their process. You protect their heart even when you have to confront something difficult.

Unforgiveness makes the heart harsh, not only toward the one who hurt you but toward everyone around you. A wounded heart becomes defensive. It reads everything as a threat. But once the heart heals, you become a vessel of grace. You bring calm into chaos, understanding into confusion, and gentleness into tension. Grace begins shaping how you love, how you parent, how you communicate, and how you see others. And because of that shift, your relationships begin to heal too.

Grace Makes You Slow to Anger and Quick to Forgive

People who have received grace give grace easily. You remember how long it took for God to heal you. You remember His patience. You remember His comfort. So when others fail, you respond differently.

You do not rush into anger because you understand the value of gentle understanding.

You do not hold grudges because you know how heavy unforgiveness feels.

You do not demand perfection because you know how fragile the human heart really is.

People who refuse to forgive often become bitter without meaning to. That bitterness spills into other relationships. But healed people break that cycle. They shape a different inheritance. They love differently. They respond differently. They create a new pattern through the grace they have learned. Their lives become safe places for others.

Grace Deepens Your Understanding of God

Something sacred happens when you heal from something that once felt impossible to survive. You begin understanding God's love in ways you never understood before. His patience becomes more meaningful. His gentleness becomes more precious. His faithfulness becomes more real. His forgiveness becomes personal.

A healed heart becomes a heart that reflects His character. You begin forgiving like Him, sometimes slowly at first, but eventually with natural compassion. You see people with understanding instead of judgment. You love with depth instead of fear. Forgiveness becomes more than a command. It becomes something God empowers within you. People who walk in grace understand God deeply because they have experienced His healing personally.

Grace Turns Your Story Into Ministry

God brings people into your life who need the very healing He has given you. Their stories may differ from yours, but their pain feels familiar. They may struggle to explain what they feel, but you understand. They may not know how to begin healing, but you know where to start. They may feel alone, but your presence becomes proof that healing is possible.

This is one of the beautiful purposes of pain. God uses what you survived as a key to someone else's freedom. Healing reveals a version of you equipped to help others. When you forgive, your heart becomes a place where others can breathe freely again. This is the ministry of the healed. God never wastes pain. What the enemy hoped would destroy you becomes something God uses to restore others. Your healed heart becomes a vessel that pours grace into those who cross your path.

Grace Gives You a New Kind of Strength

Before healing, strength looks like endurance. It looks like surviving, pushing, tolerating, and holding on. But after healing, strength becomes peace. It becomes stability. It becomes quiet confidence. It becomes unshakeable faith. It becomes the ability to stay gentle in a harsh world.

A healed heart does not brag about survival. It doesn't need to. Its strength is quiet. Its presence is steady. Its spirit is kind. Forgiveness opens the door to a strength you may not have known you had. Healing uncovers the strength that comes from God rather than self-protection. Grace strengthens you in ways pain never could.

Grace Makes You Whole Again

One of the most beautiful things about grace is the wholeness it brings. Pain once left you feeling scattered inside. You felt split between who you were and who pain made you become. Healing brings those pieces together again. You become whole. Not untouched, but restored. Not flawless, but free.

A healed heart does not pretend the pain never happened. It simply refuses to let pain decide the rest of the story. Grace becomes the final chapter, not brokenness. And in the quiet aftermath of healing, you realize you have become a carrier of grace. A living testimony. A reflection of God's mercy. A light for others still walking through their storms.

Chapter 18: Walking in Love Without Fear

F Fear is one of the quietest scars pain leaves behind. Even after forgiveness begins, even after healing starts its gentle work in you, fear can still linger like a shadow. It isn't always loud. It doesn't always shout. Sometimes it whispers. Sometimes it hides under caution. Sometimes it dresses itself up like wisdom. But fear, no matter how polished it looks, is still fear. And if love is going to flourish again, fear has to be faced.

Pain teaches the heart to protect itself. It trains you to expect hurt, anticipate disappointment, and believe vulnerability is dangerous. It builds invisible walls around the soul, walls meant to keep you safe. But over time, those same walls start feeling like prison bars. They keep danger out, but they keep love out too. They push heartache away, but they block joy as well. They silence the possibility of pain, and they also silence the possibility of connection.

Unforgiveness and hurt teach the heart to live on guard, always scanning for threat, always bracing for another wound. That kind of emotional hypervigilance drains the soul. It makes relationships exhausting. It makes affection feel unsafe. It makes vulnerability feel like walking straight into fire. Healing, especially forgiveness, begins dismantling that fear brick by brick. Little by little, the heart starts believing again that love is not the enemy.

Love Is Never Meant to Be Fearful

Fear and love can't live together in the same space. Scripture says perfect love casts out fear, and that isn't just poetic. It's truth. Love expects good. Fear expects harm. Love sees possibility. Fear sees threats. Love opens. Fear closes.

But when you've been wounded, those words can feel far away. If you trusted before and got betrayed, love feels risky. If you opened your heart and someone mishandled it, vulnerability feels foolish. If you let someone close and they used that access to hurt you, letting anyone in again can feel almost impossible.

Still, love is designed to be fearless. God doesn't create love to be something you tiptoe around. He creates it to be something you live fully. Love needs openness, trust, and presence. Those things can't grow in a heart ruled by fear. Healing gives you the courage to love again, not because you forget the past, but because you refuse to let the past decide your future.

Fear Looks Protective, But It Also Blocks You

Fear shows up like a bodyguard. It warns you not to trust. It whispers that heartbreak is waiting. It says vulnerability is dangerous. In the beginning, that can feel like protection. But eventually fear becomes restrictive. It keeps you from growing. It keeps you from intimacy. It keeps you from healthy bonds.

Pain can force you into emotional defense mode. Everyone starts looking like a threat. Every relationship feels like a risk. Over time you begin living from survival instead of purpose. You may even tell yourself you're being wise, when really you're just being afraid.

Freedom from fear doesn't come from avoiding love. It comes from healing the places where love once wounded you. Forgiveness is the first step. When you forgive, fear loses its grip. When you forgive, the voice that says never trust again starts getting quieter. When you forgive, you make space for God to rebuild confidence pain once shattered.

Love After Pain Needs Wisdom, Not Walls

Loving without fear doesn't mean ignoring wisdom. It doesn't mean trusting blindly or opening your heart carelessly. Wisdom and fear are not the same. Fear closes your heart. Wisdom guards it. Fear pushes people away. Wisdom discerns who should come close. Fear treats everyone as dangerous. Wisdom sees clearly.

Healing restores discernment. Pain makes you defensive, but healing makes you discerning. When fear leads, relationships collapse. When wisdom leads, relationships grow. Walking in love without fear means having boundaries instead of barriers. It means being open without being exposed. It means letting God guide your heart instead of letting trauma do it.

Healing Makes Love Feel Safe Again

As God heals you, something returns that you may not feel in a long time. Safety. Emotional safety. Spiritual safety. Relational safety. Safety is the soil love grows in. When your heart feels safe, it opens naturally. It loves freely. It trusts wisely. It gives without bracing for rejection.

Forgiveness frees the heart from emotional slavery, and that freedom is what makes love feel safe again. Without healing, fear stays the loudest voice. With healing, fear doesn't disappear overnight, but it stops running your life. It stops dictating decisions. It stops shaping connections. It stops defining your future.

Safety doesn't come from finding perfect people. It comes from becoming a healed version of you. When your heart heals, love starts feeling like a blessing again, not a threat.

Learning to Receive Love Again

For some people, loving others is easier than being loved. Pain convinces you that receiving love makes you weak, dependent, or exposed. You might give love freely but flinch when it comes back toward you. You might care deeply for others but doubt that you are safe enough to be cared for.

Healing changes that. It deepens your ability not only to love but to be loved. It teaches you to let others support you, encourage you, comfort you, and walk with you. It reminds you that you are worthy of love because you are God's creation, not because you are flawless.

Pain makes you believe you don't deserve love, when really you're afraid of it. Healing breaks that lie. It helps you receive love without suspicion, without fear, and without resistance. Walking in love without fear means accepting love as a gift, not as a danger.

Trusting God First Is What Makes Fearless Love Possible

Every healing journey eventually lands on this truth. The heart loves fearlessly when it trusts God fully. Not when it trusts people perfectly, but when it trusts God deeply. People can disappoint. God doesn't. When your trust is rooted in Him, you stop expecting people to carry what only He can sustain.

Forgiveness restores your relationship with God first. And when that relationship is healed, human relationships feel less threatening. If you trust God with your heart, you don't fear what people might do to it. Trusting God doesn't erase the possibility of pain, but it protects you from living afraid of pain.

Fearless Love Reflects God's Nature

God loves without fear. He loves knowing we can reject Him. He loves knowing we can fail Him. He loves knowing we can walk away. His love isn't cautious or guarded. It is generous, open, relentless, and brave.

When you walk in love without fear, you reflect His nature. You love with strength, not weakness. You love with truth, not naivety. You love with discernment, not insecurity. You love with freedom, not bondage. Fearful love is fragile. Healed love is strong.

Fearless love is mature love. It's God shaped love. It's a healed heart in motion.

Love Without Fear Is Possible Again

Walking in love without fear doesn't mean you never feel afraid. It means fear no longer leads. Fear no longer speaks first. Fear no longer decides how close you let people get. Love becomes louder. Love becomes clearer. Love becomes safer. And yes, love becomes possible again.

Chapter 19: Protecting Your Freedom (Staying Healed)

Healing isn't only something you receive. It's also something you guard. Once your heart walks through forgiveness, once God starts restoring what pain tries to destroy, once peace begins returning quietly to your soul, you have to learn how to protect that restoration. Not out of fear, but out of wisdom. Not out of suspicion, but out of reverence for what God is doing in you.

It's possible to be healed and still slip back into old wounds if you aren't paying attention. Bitterness can resurface if you leave the door open. Old thoughts, old triggers, and old emotions can creep back in if you handle them loosely. That doesn't mean your healing is weak. Your healing is a miracle. But miracles require stewardship.

Unforgiveness waits quietly for a chance to return. It hides in memories, in conversations, in moments when you feel tired or exposed. That's why healing needs tending like a garden. If you don't care for it, weeds grow back. If you nurture it, it keeps flourishing.

Freedom Needs Protection

A lot of people think once they forgive, the journey ends. But forgiveness is both a moment and a process. The decision to forgive can happen in a moment. Living in that forgiveness every day is where the work continues. You can choose forgiveness quickly, but emotional freedom is something you maintain over time.

Healed hearts are tender hearts, not fragile, but precious. And anything precious needs protection. The enemy doesn't waste energy attacking what is already broken. He aims for what is being restored. Unforgiveness often tries to creep back in through memory, and that's where the battle usually shows up first, right at the doorway of your mind. Staying free isn't only about the absence of pain. It's the discipline of remaining free.

Watch the Stories You Tell Yourself

Most battles are won or lost in the mind. Even after forgiveness, your mind can slip into old patterns. You replay conversations, imagine different outcomes, or reinterpret a past event through fear instead of truth. Old wounds try to define you again. Old identities try to return. Old insecurities whisper familiar lies.

Pain may knock again, not because it has real power, but because it remembers your old habits. But your healed heart speaks a new language now. It carries new truth and a new identity. Pain becomes a habit if you don't confront it, and habits have to be replaced. If you don't replace an old thought with a new truth, the old thought comes back stronger.

Staying healed means paying attention to what you allow your mind to revisit. If the story you repeat leads you back into bitterness, then that story needs to be challenged. Healing is protected by truth, not by memory.

Be Intentional About Emotional Boundaries

Healing often requires a fresh look at who has access to your heart. Not everyone should hold the same place they once did. Not every relationship returns to its old form. Some people can be in your life but not in your emotions. Some can be near you without being close. Some can be forgiven without being trusted.

Forgiveness isn't an invitation to let people hurt you repeatedly. Boundaries are not barriers. They are safeguards. They tell your heart where it can rest and where it needs caution. Staying healed means you don't expose your heart recklessly. You don't return to environments that once broke you. You don't reopen connections God has already closed. Wisdom protects what healing restores.

Recognize Triggers Without Surrendering to Them

Even after forgiveness, triggers can still show up. A scent, a song, a phrase, a place, or even a harmless gesture can wake up old emotions. Healing doesn't erase memory. It changes the way memory affects you.

When a trigger rises, it doesn't mean you fail. It doesn't mean you go backward. It means you're human. What matters is how quickly you return to truth. Triggers are invitations back to places you already leave. That's what they are. They pull you backward, while healing keeps inviting you forward.

So when a trigger comes, acknowledge it gently. Don't dwell. Don't spiral. Don't feed it. Bring it to God. Speak truth into it. Remind your heart that it is healed, not bound. Triggers lose their power when truth meets them head on.

Stay Close to God, the Source of Healing

Healing can involve people, but it comes from God. The moment you drift from Him, you start drifting toward the emotions that once held you captive. Staying healed means staying close to God on purpose, consistently and humbly.

Prayer steadies the heart. Worship keeps it tender. Scripture grounds it. Gratitude softens it. Emotional heaviness lifts when the heart draws near to God. Distance creates space for bitterness to return. Closeness makes bitterness harder to sustain. Protecting your healing isn't about self-reliance. It's about dependence on God.

Let Joy Back In

One of the clearest signs of healing is joy returning. But joy has to be welcomed intentionally. Pain used to train you to expect disappointment. Healing teaches you to expect goodness. Pain made you brace for impact. Healing helps you breathe freely again.

Joy doesn't force itself into your life. You open the door for it. You let yourself laugh without guilt, smile without suspicion, enjoy moments without waiting for them to fall apart. Joy is the lightness that returns after forgiveness, and it can feel fragile at first if you don't embrace it. Staying healed means you allow yourself to enjoy life without constantly looking over your shoulder. Joy is not a luxury. It's proof of freedom.

Refuse to Rehearse the Old Narrative

There will be moments when old hurts feel tempting to revisit. Pain can become nostalgic, even when it was destructive. The mind wants to argue with the past, rewrite details, or imagine different endings. But rehearsing old pain reopens old wounds.

Reliving the past keeps you stuck in the very moment you already escape. That's why forgiveness is not only letting go of the person. It's letting go of the story that chains you to the wound. You can't control every memory that comes, but you can choose not to entertain it. You can't stop every thought, but you can stop nourishing the ones that drag you backward. To stay healed, you let the past stay in the past.

Embrace Who You Are Becoming

Healing changes you. Not into someone unfamiliar, but into someone truer. Someone wiser, gentler, stronger, freer, and more compassionate. You start discovering parts of yourself pain buried. You uncover joy you forgot existed. You break patterns you once think were permanent. You walk in confidence instead of caution. You speak from truth instead of trauma.

Healing doesn't only return you to who you were before pain. Sometimes it grows you into an even better version. Staying healed means you embrace that person without apology, without fear, and without shrinking back. You are not who you were before the wound. You are stronger. You are not who pain tries to make you. You are healed. Protect that healing with everything you have.

Staying Healed Is Worship

Protecting your healing isn't selfish. It's obedience. It honors what God has done. It recognizes that your freedom costs something, your surrender, your tears, your willingness, and His grace. Staying healed is worship because it's gratitude in motion. It says, I will not waste what You restore. I will not return to what You deliver me from. I will not reopen what You close.

Healing is God's gift. Protecting it is your responsibility. Living in it is your testimony. As you keep walking forward with the peace that once felt impossible, you become living proof that forgiveness works, healing is real, and freedom is possible.

Chapter 20: The Healed Life: When God Writes the Ending

There comes a moment in every healing journey when you look back and realize you are not the same person who once cried, trembled, questioned, and wondered if peace would ever return. You see how far God brings you, how deeply He touches the parts of you no one else can reach, and how beautifully He redeems what once feels beyond repair. This is the healed life. It isn't a perfect life. It isn't a life with no memories. It's a life where pain no longer defines you, directs you, or diminishes you.

Healing doesn't erase your story. It changes what the story means. Forgiveness lets God take the pen from your trembling hands and write something new, something you could never write on your own. The healed life is the proof that God takes what feels meant for destruction and turns it into something that carries His glory.

The Healed Life Lives in Freedom, Not Fear

When the heart heals, fear starts losing its grip. You stop anticipating hurt around every corner. You stop expecting disappointment as your default. You stop assuming the worst about people and moments. You stop living in emotional defense mode all the time. The healed life is a free life. Free from the slavery of unforgiveness. Free from the bitterness that eats away at peace. Free from memories that once hijack joy.

Freedom doesn't mean you forget what happens. It means the memory no longer torments you. You remember without reliving. The story stays, but the sting fades. The moment exists, but it stops owning you. When forgiveness takes root, the heart breathes again, and that breathing feels deep and steady, not shallow and fearful. That is the healed life, unburdened and unafraid.

The Healed Life Sees God Everywhere

Looking back after healing, you start seeing God's fingerprints all over the journey. You see how He protects you from breaking completely. You see how He carries you when you are falling apart. You see how He whispers truth when lies are loud. You see how He guides you step by step, even when you don't understand what He's doing.

Pain can convince you that God is distant, but healing shows you He is close, especially in the valley. You recognize Him in tears, in silence, in surrender, and in the stillness of letting go. Healing brings spiritual clarity, and your eyes open to the truth that God never abandons His own. The healed life sees God not as the author of pain, but as the restorer of the heart.

The Healed Life Loves Without Carrying Old Baggage

When healing blooms, love becomes easier, not because people suddenly become perfect, but because you are different. You don't love from fear anymore. You don't measure affection through old wounds. You don't project yesterday's disappointments onto today's relationships. You love from a healed place, not a wounded one.

This is one of the quiet beauties of healing. You rediscover tenderness. You rediscover courage. You rediscover the joy of giving and receiving love without dragging the weight of the past into every moment. Forgiveness doesn't make you reckless. It makes you free. You trust again, wisely. You open up again, with strength. The healed life loves openly, but with discernment shaped by God.

The Healed Life Walks in Purpose

Pain can make you forget who you are. It can blur your identity. It can shrink your dreams and quiet your goals. It can make you believe your story is too broken to be useful. Healing restores purpose. It wakes up the calling pain tries to bury.

You start dreaming again. You start pursuing again. You start believing again. You begin to see your story as something that carries weight, spiritual weight, emotional weight, kingdom weight. God does not waste pain. Every tear becomes soil for purpose. Every wound becomes a testimony. Every heartbreak becomes something God can use to minister to others.

The healed life shows that your purpose gets clearer as your heart gets clearer. God uses healed people to heal others. He uses restored hearts to guide broken hearts. He uses your journey to light someone else's path. Pain no longer controls you. Instead, it starts propelling you forward.

The Healed Life Has Boundaries That Guard Peace

Healing doesn't erase the need for boundaries. If anything, it deepens your respect for them. Not because you are afraid, but because you understand what your peace costs. You recognize your heart is worth protecting. You understand not everyone deserves the same level of access. You see that healing can be damaged if wisdom is neglected.

Healing teaches you who to let in and who to release. Boundaries become a form of gratitude. They say, God restores me, and I refuse to return to what breaks me. They protect the healed version of you. They preserve your peace. They honor your journey. They keep what God rebuilds from being torn down again.

The Healed Life Becomes a Living Testimony

People who know you in your broken season will see the difference. They will hear it in your words. They will feel it in your presence. They will notice it in your reactions, your choices, and your posture. Healing changes you from the inside out, and that change becomes hard to miss. The healed life doesn't need to announce itself. It shines.

Your healed life becomes evidence. It becomes a sermon without a microphone. It becomes a testimony without a script. God uses healed hearts like lanterns. They light up dark places, guide others toward hope, and show what redemption looks like in real life.

The Healed Life Trusts God With the Future

One of the deepest signs of the healed life is trust, not trust in people, but trust in God. You stop fearing what lies ahead. You stop bracing for disappointment as if it's guaranteed. You stop catastrophizing small moments. You walk with a quiet assurance that whatever comes, God will sustain you.

Pain makes you uncertain. Healing makes you confident, not in a loud way, but in a peaceful way. You trust that God turns mourning into dancing, ashes into beauty, sorrow into joy. And if He restores you once, He remains faithful to do it again. Healing helps you see that God is writing something bigger the entire time, even in seasons when you feel lost or abandoned.

The Ending Is Restoration, Not the Wound

As this chapter of your journey closes, you stand at the edge of a new beginning. The wound is part of your story, but it is not the end. The hurt matters, but it is not final. The pain shapes you, but it does not define you. Forgiveness frees you. Healing restores you. God completes the work.

The healed life is not a return to who you are before the pain. It is the unveiling of who you are becoming. Someone wiser, kinder, stronger, softer, freer, and more like Christ. The end of your story is not what happens to you. The end is what God does in you. He gathers the pieces pain tries to scatter. He holds them gently. He restores them faithfully. He breathes life into them again.

Your healed life is the evidence. Your healed life is the testimony. Your healed life is the miracle. God writes the ending, and it is more beautiful than anything pain ever predicts.

Conclusion: You Are Proof That Healing Is Possible

T here is something sacred about reaching the end of a journey that once feels impossible to begin. When you first hold this book, your heart might feel heavy. Maybe you are wounded, confused, or exhausted. Maybe you carry pain for months, years, or even decades. Maybe you wonder if healing is even possible for someone like you, someone who already survives so much. But as you turn these final pages, I pray you see what I see, a heart that is softened, strengthened, reshaped, and touched by the hand of God.

You walk a road many people avoid. You face truths you bury. You confront memories that once tighten your chest. You wrestle with emotions that feel too overwhelming to hold. And through all of it, you choose courage instead of fear, honesty instead of denial, surrender instead of control, forgiveness instead of bitterness, and healing instead of hiding.

Your original pain may not vanish, but something extraordinary happens. Your heart changes. The wound no longer owns you. The story no longer binds you. Fear no longer governs you. You are no longer the version of yourself shaped by hurt. You are the version shaped by grace.

You Don't Walk Alone

Healing can feel lonely at times, but you never walk alone. God is with you in the beginning, before you have the strength to name the hurt. God is with you in the middle, when forgiveness feels impossible. God is with you in quiet moments, the nights you cry silently, the mornings you question everything, the days when memories rise unexpectedly. And God is with you now, right here at this point of closure.

Healing is proof of God's nearness, not His distance. When you look back, you start seeing His fingerprints everywhere. You see how He sustains you, refines you, and strengthens you. You see how every moment of pain becomes a place for His presence to rest on you. This road is never walked by your strength alone. It is walked by surrender, and God meets you in every surrender.

You Are Not Going Back

Here is one of the most important truths to hold as you finish this book. You are not going back. You are not returning to old habits, old thoughts, old emotions, or old versions of yourself. You are not returning to cycles of unforgiveness. You are not returning to patterns that break you. You are not returning to the heaviness that once shapes your days. You are not returning to relationships that destroy your peace. You are not returning to the prison you just leave.

It is easy to slip into emotional looping, replaying the past as if it still holds power. But now you know the truth. The moment you forgive, the past loses its hold. The hurt loses its authority. The memory loses its sting. You owe your past nothing. You owe your future everything. You move forward lighter, freer, wiser, and stronger.

You Are Becoming Who God Intends You to Be

Healing always leads to transformation. You may feel different now. You may think differently, walk differently, love differently, and pray differently. That is not accidental. God is reshaping you. He is restoring the parts pain buries, reviving pieces that feel dead, and waking strengths you don't even know you carry.

Confidence returns. Hope renews. Joy is reborn. You are becoming yourself again, not the guarded version, not the fearful version, not the broken version, but the person God sees before pain enters the story. Healing doesn't just return you to who you were. Healing reveals who you are.

Your Story Has Purpose

There is something beautiful about a healed heart. It becomes a well of wisdom for others. Your story turns into a mirror where someone else sees hope. Your scars become a map for people still trying to find their way out of their own wounds. What once feels like the most painful part of your life becomes the testimony God uses to bring healing to others.

Pain teaches compassion, and healing teaches grace. Because of what you survive, you now carry both. You become gentle with others because you know what it feels like to break. You become patient because you know healing can be slow. You become discerning because you learn to notice silent suffering. You become compassionate because God is compassionate to you.

Never underestimate the impact of a healed heart. It shines

without trying. It speaks without forcing words. It lifts people without even realizing it. It touches lives because it carries the fragrance of grace.

You Are Walking Into a New Season

This isn't the end of your healing. It is the beginning of your healed life. You keep growing, changing, softening, and strengthening. Healing is not a destination. It is a lifelong unfolding of God's goodness in your heart. As you step into this new season, you begin noticing transformation everywhere.

Conversations feel lighter. Relationships feel healthier. Memories feel less sharp. Thoughts feel clearer. Your heart feels more open. Your mind feels more peaceful. Your steps feel more confident. This is the fruit of forgiveness. This is the evidence of healing. This is God's grace working in you.

God Is Still Working

You reach the end of this book, but you do not reach the end of God's work in your life. Healing continues. Growth continues. Wisdom deepens. Love expands. Peace strengthens. You become even more whole, more grounded, and more radiant.

And when life brings new challenges, you meet them differently now. You don't respond from the wound but from the healed place. You don't move from fear but from faith. You don't act from insecurity but from identity. You don't live from pain but from purpose. Healing is proof that God is writing your story, and He still is.

You Are Proof

You are proof that forgiveness is possible. You are proof that healing is real. You are proof that God restores. You are proof that pain does not get the final word. You are proof that wounds can become testimonies. You are proof that grace wins over bitterness. You are proof that love survives loss. You are proof that a human heart can rise again.

Your story matters. Your healing matters. Your life matters. People will be touched by the healed version of you. This is your new beginning. Step into it boldly. Walk forward freely. Live fully, joyfully, deeply, and on purpose, because you are healed. And your healed life is a chapter God will use to heal many others.

10-DAY Prayer Journey

Day 1, A Prayer to Begin Healing

Father, I come before You with a heart that is worn, heavy, and honest. You see the places within me that I have tried to hide from others and even from myself. You know the wounds that have shaped me and the memories that still live inside me. Today, I release the fear of approaching this journey. I surrender the walls I have built to protect myself. I ask You to meet me at this beginning, not with judgment, but with grace. Heal the parts of me I have numbed. Touch the places I am afraid to revisit. Give me courage to confront what I have buried and strength to walk through what has held me captive. I invite You into the deepest rooms of my heart. Lead me gently, Lord, and assure me that as I begin this healing, I do not walk alone. Amen.

Day 2, A Prayer for Honesty About the Hurt

Lord, I confess that some of my pain is older than I want to admit. Some wounds still ache, though I have tried to convince myself that I moved on. Today, I ask for the courage to be honest. Help me speak the truth of how much this hurt, how deeply it cut, and how silently I bled. Peel back every layer of denial. Expose the places I have tried to patch with distractions. Give me the freedom to name the pain without shame. And as I acknowledge what happened, remind me that You are not shocked by my story. You are the God who sees, the God who understands, and the God who heals. Let honesty be the beginning of breakthrough. Amen.

Day 3, A Prayer for Strength to Forgive

Heavenly Father, forgiveness feels impossible some days. My emotions resist it. My mind argues against it. My heart clings to its pain. But today,

I choose Your way over my way. Give me the strength to forgive, even before I feel like it. Help me realize that forgiveness is not approval of the wrong but release from the weight of it. I do not want to be chained to anger, bitterness, resentment, or revenge. Give me the courage to say, "I forgive," even if my voice trembles. Meet me in this decision. Empower me to obey You first, knowing that healing will follow. Make forgiveness the path where freedom begins. Amen.

Day 4, A Prayer for the Softening of My Heart

Lord, my heart has grown guarded. Pain made me cautious, careful, and afraid. I have protected myself so fiercely that I forgot how to let love in. Today, I ask You to soften the hardened places within me. Remove the emotional armor that has kept others at a distance. Heal the suspicion, dissolve the tension, and quiet the fear. Replace my defensiveness with discernment. Replace my walls with healthy boundaries. Teach my heart to feel again, to trust again, to hope again, to love again. Let Your gentleness reshape me and restore the tenderness I thought I lost forever. Amen.

Day 5, A Prayer for the Person Who Hurt Me

Father, today I pray for the one who hurt me. This prayer is difficult, but I choose obedience over comfort. I do not pray from bitterness; I pray from surrender. You know their story. You know their wounds. You know their weaknesses, their fears, and their broken places. I release the desire for revenge. I release the expectation of an apology. I release the hope that they will ever fully understand my pain. Bless them, Lord, not because they deserve it, but because I refuse to let hatred live in my heart. I place them in Your hands, knowing You alone are the righteous Judge. Let this prayer be the final loosening of the chains that once bound us. Amen.

Day 6, A Prayer for Release From the Past

Lord Jesus, the past has held onto me longer than I wanted it to. Memories return when I least expect them. Old emotions rise like waves. Sometimes the past feels louder than the present. Today, I ask for divine release. Break the ties that still connect me to what happened. Lift the weight of every memory that brings pain. Silence the voice of shame. Dismantle the lies that were formed in moments of hurt. Give me the courage to stop rehearsing the story in my mind. Teach me to look forward without constantly glancing backward. I place the past at Your feet, every moment, every tear, every wound. Set me free from it completely. Amen.

Day 7, A Prayer for a Renewed Identity

Father, for too long pain has influenced how I see myself. It has made me feel smaller, weaker, and less deserving. But today, I receive Your truth over my identity. I am not what happened to me. I am not the scar, the betrayal, or the disappointment. I am who You say I am, chosen, beloved, valued, and restored. Help me rediscover the version of myself that pain tried to bury. Restore my confidence. Renew my self-worth. Heal my self-image. Make me whole again in the way only You can. Let the healed version of me rise with dignity and strength. Amen.

Day 8, A Prayer for Wisdom and Boundaries

Lord, healing has made my heart soft again, but I do not want to be unprotected. Teach me the difference between walls and boundaries. Give me wisdom to discern who should walk closely with me and who should remain at a distance. Help me recognize what environments nurture my healing and which ones threaten it. Give me the strength to say no without guilt. Give me the maturity to say yes without fear. And above all, surround me with relationships that reflect Your love, Your safety, and Your peace. Guard my heart as I guard it with You. Amen.

Day 9, A Prayer for New Joy

Father, joy once felt impossible. Pain made happiness feel foreign. But today, I open my heart to joy again. Not temporary joy, not shallow joy, but the deep, peaceful joy that comes from You. Restore laughter to my soul. Restore lightness to my steps. Restore excitement to my future. Let joy be my strength, my atmosphere, my inheritance. And let the joy You place in me become a testimony to those still waiting for their healing. Fill me with joy that overflows, gentle, steady, and pure. Amen.

Day 10, A Prayer to Walk Forward in Freedom

God of healing, God of restoration, God of new beginnings, today I thank You for what You have done in my heart. I am not who I was when this journey began. Something within me has shifted. Something has opened. Something has healed. I step into this new season without fear, without bitterness, without regret. I walk forward in freedom, knowing that You are the One who healed me, the One who restored me, and the One who carries me. Protect my peace. Strengthen my boundaries. Deepen my joy. Expand my love. And let my life be a living testimony that forgiveness works, healing is possible, and You are faithful. Amen

www.ingramcontent.com/pod-product-compliance
Lightning Source LLC
Chambersburg PA
CBHW031534040426
42445CB00010B/529